I0150123

The Superior Foundation of the King James Bible

By Pastor D. A. Waite, Th.D., Ph.D.
Bible For Today Baptist Church

the
BIBLE
FOR
TODAY

900 Park Avenue
Collingswood, NJ 08108
Phone: 856-854-4452
www.BibleForToday.org

BFT #3384

Published by

THE BIBLE FOR TODAY PRESS
900 Park Avenue
Collingswood, New Jersey 08108
U.S.A.

Church Phone: 856-854-4747
BFT Phone: 856-854-4452
Orders: 1-800-John 10:9
e-mail: BFT@BibleForToday.org
Website: www.BibleForToday.org
fax: 856-854-2464

We Use and Defend
the King James Bible

November, 2008
BFT 3384

Copyright, 2008
All Rights Reserved

ISBN #1-56848-062-8

Acknowledgments

**I wish to thank and to acknowledge the assistance
of the following people:**

Yvonne Sanborn Waite, my wife, who encouraged the publication of this booklet, read the manuscript several times, suggested the various boxes, and gave other helpful suggestions and comments;

Julia Monaghan, a faithful supporter of our Bible For Today and Dean Burgon Society ministries, and a faithful attender via the Internet of our 𝕭𝖎𝖇𝖑𝖊 𝕱𝖔𝖗 𝕿𝖔𝖉𝖆𝖞 𝕭𝖆𝖕𝖙𝖎𝖘𝖙 𝕮𝖍𝖚𝖗𝖈𝖍 services, who read the manuscript and gave helpful comments and suggestions for revisions.

Barbara Egan, our Bible For Today secretary who proofread the manuscript and, as usual, offered valuable suggestions and comments.

Daniel S. Waite, the Assistant to the Bible For Today Director, who kept my computer working, guided the book through the printing process, and made important suggestions.

Dr. H. D. Williams, a friend and supporter of the Bible For Today and the Dean Burgon Society ministries. His expertise in "print on demand" (POD) technology has made it possible for us to print this book in this manner, thus saving us thousands of dollars. Both he and his wife, Patricia, have constructed the cover of this booklet, and have guided it through the POD publishers.

𝕱𝖔𝖗𝖊𝖜𝖔𝖗𝖉

- **The Background of This Booklet.** The idea for this booklet came from my book, *Defending The King James Bible* (**BFT #1594 @ $12.00 + $4.00 S&H**). In this book, I point out four superiorities of the King James Bible: It has (1) superior texts, (2) superior translators, (3) superior translation technique, and (4) superior theology. I have simply taken point #1 and edited it for printing here.

- **The Need For This Booklet.** One of the most important parts of the battle for the real Bible in our time is the answer to the question: Which Old Testament Hebrew and Aramaic Words and which New Testament Greek Words are we to use as the basis for all our translations? Since there are so many viewpoints on this, there is a drastic need to discuss the problem in detail.

- **The Purpose of This Booklet.** In this booklet, I attempt to meet the need to talk about this matter and to give my reasons why I believe that the Hebrew, Aramaic, and Greek Words underlying the King James Bible are the only Words that should be used as the basis for Bible translations. Though it is a complex subject, I hope I might make it clear to the readers.

- **The Use of This Booklet.** I will be using this booklet at two upcoming meetings. One meeting will be at an independent Baptist college. The other will be at a Bible conference in Mexico. I hope it will be used by hundreds and even thousands of God's people who need answers to this vitally important problem.

> **Sincerely Yours For God's Words,**
> **Pastor D. A. Waite, Th.D., Ph.D.**
> **𝕭𝖎𝖇𝖑𝖊 𝕱𝖔𝖗 𝕿𝖔𝖉𝖆𝖞 𝕭𝖆𝖕𝖙𝖎𝖘𝖙 𝕮𝖍𝖚𝖗𝖈𝖍**

Table of Contents

THE KING JAMES BIBLE IS GOD'S WORDS KEPT INTACT IN ENGLISH BECAUSE OF ITS SUPERIOR ORIGINAL LANGUAGE WORDS

By Pastor D. A. Waite, Th.D., Ph.D.
Bible For Today Baptist Church

Introductory Comments

In Chapter II of my book, *Defending the King James Bible* (**BFT #1594 @ $12.00 + $4.00 S&H**), I listed four reasons why the King James Bible is superior to all other English versions. The first of these four reasons is its superior Hebrew, Aramaic, and Greek Words. The other three superiorities are its superior translators, its superior translation technique, and its superior theology. This booklet will deal with one of the four reasons why God's Words are kept intact best in English in the King James Bible. It is because of its superior Hebrew, Aramaic, and Greek Words from which it was translated.

The task of looking into the Hebrew, Aramaic and Greek Words in which our Bible was originally written is a technical and difficult one. However, it would be helpful if every Bible-believing Christian would wade through this material and seek to learn as much as possible about it.

I firmly believe that the Hebrew, Aramaic, and Greek Words that underlie our King James Bible have been preserved for us right down to the present day. I believe that Bible preservation must be related to and integrated with Bible inspiration. Our omnipotent God originally gave us our Bible in Words that were verbally and plenarily inspired. It is both Scriptural and reasonable that this same omnipotent God would guard those verbally, plenarily inspired Words by the verbal, plenary preservation of those Words.

In the next pages, I will try to show that the Hebrew, Aramaic, and Greek Words underlying the King James Bible are the very original Hebrew,

Aramaic, and Greek Words that God gave us in the first place. This sound position is a minority position in the days in which we live, but it is a Biblical position. Modern versions in all the languages of the world have used a different set of Hebrew and Aramaic words for their Old Testament basis and also a different set of Greek words for their New Testament basis. This is a serious and confusing situation.

Though some of our Fundamentalist brethren who hold to the critical Greek text strongly disagree (and have written books about their disagreement). There are many important differences between the critical and the traditional Greek texts. Some of these differences involve important doctrines. Dr. Jack Moorman has spent hundreds of hours in preparing his book entitled *8,000 Differences Between the N.T. Greek Words of the King James Bible and the Modern Versions* (**BFT #3084 @ $20.00 + $5.00 S&H**). Some of these differences are minor, but many of them are major. In fact, over 356 passages in the critical Greek text are doctrinal in nature. These passages are clearly outlined by Dr. Jack Moorman in his excellent book, *Early Versions, Church Fathers, and the Authorized Version* (**BFT #3230 @ $20.00 + $5.00 S&H**).

I hope the readers will be armed with some important facts about the Hebrew, Aramaic, and Greek foundations of the modern Bible versions as compared with the foundation of our King James Bible. As our readers read this booklet, I hope that they do not give up when they come to difficult parts of it. Please keep reading. Ask the Lord to help you to understand this important subject concerning God's precious Words..

I. THE KING JAMES BIBLE IS GOD'S WORDS KEPT INTACT IN ENGLISH BECAUSE OF ITS SUPERIOR OLD TESTAMENT HEBREW WORDS

The KING JAMES BIBLE is translated from **superior** Old Testament Words. It is translated from what we call the Traditional Masoretic Hebrew Old Testament text edited by Jacob ben Chayyim. The other versions that are translated today, such as the NEW AMERICAN STANDARD VERSION of 1960, the NEW INTERNATIONAL VERSION of 1969, the NEW KING JAMES VERSION of 1979, and the other modern versions use questionable Hebrew and Aramaic words. They make use of a text edited by Ben Asher rather than by Ben Chayyim. The word, "*Masoretic*," comes from *masor,* a Hebrew word meaning "*traditional.*"

The Masoretes

The Masoretes handed down this text from generation to generation. They guarded it and kept it well, as we will see.

A. The Inferior Old Testament Words of the New Versions.

1. The NEW AMERICAN STANDARD VERSION'S Old Testament Words.

Take a look, for instance, at the NEW AMERICAN STANDARD VERSION (NASV). The editors admit, in their Preface (p. viii), the following:

> "Hebrew Text: In the present translation the latest edition of **[1] Rudolph Kittel's BIBLIA HEBRAICA** has been employed together with the most recent **[2] light from**

lexicography, [3] cognate languages, and [4] the Dead Sea Scrolls."

You can see from this that the NASV does not use exclusively the Masoretic Hebrew Text (the right one), but makes use of other sources as well. The Hebrew text they use is Kittel's *BIBLIA HEBRAICA*. That would be the 1937 edition, the same one we used when I studied Hebrew under Dr. Merrill Frederick Unger at Dallas Theological Seminary (1948-53).

20,000–30,000 Suggested Changes

This edition has about fifteen to twenty suggested changes in the Hebrew text placed in the footnotes on each page. If you multiply 15 or 20 by the 1424 pages in this Kittel Bible, it comes out to between 20,000 and almost 30,000 suggested footnote changes in the Old Testament. They could be major changes, or they could be minor changes. Does that sound like a *"preserved"* Bible to you? Does that sound like the fulfillment of the promise of the Lord Jesus Christ that not *"one jot or one tittle"* would *"pass from the law till all be fulfilled"*? (Matthew 5:18)

I don't agree with the way these editors have dealt with the Old Testament text. My Saviour said that every Word, every letter, and every part of every letter would be preserved, by the power of God, until *"all be fulfilled"* (Matthew 5:18). All has not yet been *"fulfilled"* so His promise of verbal, plenary preservation of His Words has not been abrogated in any way. Evangelicals and even Fundamentalists are using and recommending the NEW AMERICAN STANDARD VERSION (NASV), the NEW INTERNATIONAL VERSION (NIV), the NEW KING JAMES VERSION (NKJV), and other modern versions all of which use inferior Old Testament words.

2. The NEW INTERNATIONAL VERSION'S

Old Testament Words. The NEW INTERNATIONAL VERSION (NIV) has a similar thing to say about its Old Testament foundation that they have used for their translation. On pages viii-ix of the NEW INTERNATIONAL VERSION of 1978, the editors wrote:

> *(p. viii) "For the Old Testament, the standard Hebrew text, the Masoretic text, as published in the latest editions of [1]* **BIBLIA HEBRAICA** [which is the same Kittel Bible I mentioned before] *was used throughout. The [2]* **DEAD SEA SCROLLS** *contain material bearing on an earlier stage of*

the Hebrew text. [So they're going to use the Dead Sea Scrolls. They're going to change it when the Dead Sea Scrolls say change it in various places]. *They were consulted as were the [3]* **SAMARITAN PENTATEUCH** [that is another text that is different from the Hebrew] *and the [4]* **ANCIENT SCRIBAL TRADITIONS** *relating to [p. ix] textual changes* [that is a tradition, maybe, in some places, and they're going to use that perhaps over the Masoretic Hebrew text for textual changes]. *Sometimes a [5]* **VARIANT HEBREW READING IN THE MARGIN** *of the Masoretic text was followed instead of the text itself. . . .* [Now they're going to use marginal readings instead of the actual text]. *In rare cases, [6]* **WORDS IN THE CONSONANTAL TEXTS WERE DIVIDED DIFFERENTLY** *from the way they appear in the Masoretic Text. . . . The translators also consulted the more important [7]* **EARLY VERSIONS**--[that is] *the [8]* **SEPTUAGINT**; [so here's the Old Testament translated into Greek and they're going to use that as their basis and foundation] *[9]* **SYMMACHUS** *and [10]* **THEODOTION** [they had a translation from the Old Testament Hebrew into Greek]; *the [11]* **VULGATE** [there's your Latin translation]; *the [12]* **SYRIAC PESHITTA**; *the [13]* **TARGUMS** *and for the Psalms, the [14]* **JUXTA HEBRAICA** *of Jerome. Readings from these versions were occasionally followed. . . . Some words were read with a [15]* **DIFFERENT SET OF VOWELS**. *These instances are usually* **NOT** *indicated by footnotes."* [My words are in brackets]. *[NIV, Preface, pp. viii-ix].*

The NIV editors have very honestly and boldly altered the Hebrew and Aramaic foundation of our Old Testament Words in the above fifteen different ways, whenever they wished to do so. You don't know at what point they have used one document or another to contradict the Traditional Masoretic Hebrew Words. It is like not being sure whether they have used cement or sand for the foundation of their version. They may have used a little cement, but all of a sudden there is much sand. You don't know whether it will hold up as a building or whether it will fall flat. Their foundation is different and defective. It has been altered.

3. The NEW KING JAMES VERSION'S Old Testament Words.

The NKJV's Mixed O.T. Base

But you might say, "*The NEW KING JAMES VERSION (NKJV) translators, are more fundamental people. They wouldn't dare change the Traditional Old Testament Words, would they?*"

Let us take a look and see what they say about their Old Testament Hebrew and Aramaic words.

The Preface of the NEW KING JAMES VERSION on page vi says
". . . *the text used was the [1] 1967/77 STUTTGART EDITION of BIBLIA HEBRAICA.*"

This is not Kittel's *Biblia Hebraica* but a new edition. I have that Hebrew text also. It is called "*Biblia Hebraica Stuttgartensia*" (which is from Stuttgart, Germany). This is similar to Kittel's edition. The date, however, is not 1937, but 1967/77. I am told that is the Hebrew text that is being used in the colleges and seminaries today. It is the one now available on computer. It can be purchased from the LOGOS Bible Study Software for Microsoft Windows and in many other places.

Two Dangerous Hebrew Bibles

The *Biblia Hebraica* from Rudolf Kittel is abbreviated BHK (*Biblia Hebraica Kittel*). The one used by the NKJV is abbreviated BHS (*Biblia Hebraica Stuttgartensia*). The BHS has a similar footnote arrangement as Kittel's.

The Ben Asher Hebrew words (though not exactly the same Hebrew Words as the ones which underlie the KING JAMES BIBLE) are printed at the top of each page. The same things holds true for this Hebrew text as for Kittel's, that is, there are still about fifteen to twenty suggested changes in the Hebrew text placed in the footnotes on each page.

Suggested Footnote O.T. Changes

This amounts also to about 20,000 to almost 30,000 suggested changes in the footnotes throughout the Old Testament.

In addition to this woefully and tragically inadequate Hebrew text, the NEW KING JAMES BIBLE preface says (p. vi):

". . . *with frequent [2] comparisons being made with the BOMBERG EDITION of 1525* [which was the basis of the KING JAMES, by the way] *the [3] SEPTUAGINT version of the Old Testament and the [4] LATIN VULGATE, in addition referring to a variety of [5] ANCIENT VERSIONS of the Hebrew Scripture and manuscripts from the [6] Dead Sea Scrolls.*" [My words in brackets].

Here is the evidence that at least six foundations were consulted and possibly used by the editors as a basis for the NKJV as their Old Testament foundation rather than exclusively the Traditional Hebrew Words.

Modern Versions–A Different Base

So you have, in all three of these Bibles that fundamental Christians are using today, Hebrew and Aramaic words and an Old Testament foundation that is different from that of the KING JAMES BIBLE. If you have a different foundation, how can the building (the Words) be the same? They can't be the same. They are not the same. They are different.

B. The Old Testament Hebrew Words Were Accumulated by the Jews. Let us take a

look at the Old Testament of the KING JAMES BIBLE and why I believe that it has a superior text. First, it was **accumulated** by the Jews, and secondly, it was **authorized** by the Lord Jesus Christ.

1. In Romans 3:1-2, We See That The Jews Were Named by God to Be the Guardians of the Old Testament Words.

The Jews Gave Us the Bible

A Scripture text that shows clearly that the Jews were the God-appointed custodians of the Old Testament Words is Romans 3:1-2. No Gentile was to put his unclean hands upon God's Old Testament Words.

I believe that even the New Testament (despite doubts by some that one book is an exception to this) was written by Jews. They are God's ancient earthly people who one day will be led to genuine faith in the Lord Jesus Christ as their Saviour. This will take place when they see their Messiah and will look upon Him "*Whom they have pierced.*" (Zechariah 12:10).

> ***Rom. 3:1-2:*** *"What advantage then hath the Jew? or what profit is there of circumcision? Much every way: chiefly, because that UNTO THEM WERE COMMITTED THE ORACLES OF GOD."*

Strong gives this information about the word, "*oracles*":

> *"3051. logion {log'-ee-on}; neuter of 3052; an utterance (of God): -oracle.*

The "*oracles of God*" are the very "*utterances*" or Words of God. Unto them (the Jews) "*were committed the oracles of God.*" This is why I place so much confidence in the traditional Masoretic Hebrew Old Testament Words that those Jews guarded and kept for us. That is why the King James translators used these Words as the basis for their Bible rather than:

(1) the Latin Vulgate (which is not Hebrew);

(2) the Septuagint Greek (which is not Hebrew);

(3) Symmachus (which is not Hebrew);

(4) Theodotion (which is not Hebrew) ;

(5) an ancient tribal tradition (which is not Hebrew's original Words);

(6) any other source which is not the traditional Masoretic Hebrew Words.

None of these other things should ever have a say in how the Words should read, nor should any of them be used to contradict the traditional Masoretic Hebrew Words that underlie the King James Bible.

2. The Methods of the Old Testament

Guardians. Let us take a look at how the Jews fulfilled this Biblical promise by their strict rules in copying the Hebrew Old Testament Words. This is from *General Biblical Introduction* by H. S. Miller (written in 1960, pages 184-185.)

He lists eight rules the Jews used in the copying of the Words from the Synagogue Rolls of the Old Testament Scriptures. These rules are mentioned in the Talmud:

1. *The parchment must be made from the skin of clean animals; must be prepared by a Jew only, and the skins must be fastened together by strings taken from clean animals.*

2. *Each column must have no less than 48 nor more than 60 lines. The entire copy must be first lined.*

3. *The ink must be of no other color than black, and it must be prepared according to a special recipe.*

4 *.No word nor letter could be written from memory; the scribe must have an authentic copy before him, and he must read and pronounce aloud each word before writing it.*

[For instance "*In the beginning God created the heaven and the earth*" You would have to pronounce the word "in the beginning" in Hebrew, (*b'reshith*); "God," (*Elohim*); "created," (*bara*); "the heaven" (*eth hashamaim*); "and the earth" (*wa eth ha arets*). He had to pronounce every word before he wrote it down, with an authentic copy before him. He had to pronounce it aloud, not just see it in his mind. This was to avoid any errors, duplications, omissions, etc.].

5. *He must reverently wipe his pen each time before writing the word for "God"* [which is *Elohim*] *and he must wash his whole body before writing the name "Jehovah"* [which is translated "LORD" in our KING JAMES BIBLE] *lest the Holy Name be contaminated.*

6. *Strict rules were given concerning forms of the letters, spaces between letters, words, and sections, the use of the pen, the color of the parchment, etc.*

7. *The revision of a roll must be made within 30 days after the work was finished; otherwise it was worthless. One mistake on a sheet condemned the sheet; if three mistakes were found on any page, the entire manuscript was condemned.*

[What if a scribe went from Genesis through to Malachi and found three mistakes? He would have to start from Genesis and go all the way to Malachi once again. From this rule you see the meticulousness with which the Jews were ordered to guard the Words of God.

Those men believed that the Words they were copying were God's holy Words. Because of this, they guarded them, unlike translators today who either add, subtract, or change in other ways the Words of God. This has been done in the NASV, NIV, NKJV, ESV, RSV, NRSV and many other modern versions. To the extent and in the places where their translators have done any of these things, they can rightly be called perversions of the truth of the Bible.]

8.   *Every word and every letter was counted,*

[Notice that the "*words*" and even the "*letters*" were counted. Think of counting all the words and letters on every page of the Hebrew Old Testament. Talk about exactness! Yet that was the method God used to preserve the Words of the Hebrew Old Testament.]

and if a letter were omitted, an extra letter inserted, or if one letter touched another, the manuscript was condemned and destroyed at once." (Miller, *op. cit.*, pp. 184-185) [My comments in brackets.]

Preserved Hebrew Words

These are historic rules the Jews used. Miller also added these words which we should bear in mind:

"Some of these rules may appear extreme and absurd, yet they show how sacred the Holy Word of the Old Testament was to its custodians, the Jews (Rom. 3:2), and they give us strong encouragement to believe that WE HAVE THE REAL OLD TESTAMENT, THE SAME ONE WHICH OUR LORD HAD AND WHICH WAS ORIGINALLY GIVEN BY INSPIRATION OF GOD." [Miller, op. cit., p. 185]

3.   A Brief History of the Traditional Hebrew Masoretic Old Testament Words. Let us take a brief look at the history of the Hebrew Old Testament Words.

The Meaning of "Masoretic"

"Masoretic," is from the Hebrew *masar ("to hand down").* It means *"to hand down from person to person."* The Masoretes were *"traditionalists"* who guarded the Old Testament Hebrew Words. There were families of Hebrew scholars in Babylon, in Palestine, and in Tiberius.

According to most students of these matters, these Masoretes safeguarded the consonantal text. According to some fundamentalist writers, the Hebrew vowels were present in the Hebrew Words right from the start. All the Masoretes had to do was to guard both consonants and vowels and keep them without change. I agree with this position. Dr. Thomas Strouse has written extensively proving that the vowels were a part of the original Hebrew Old Testament.

The Need For Hebrew Vowels

For instance, in our English language, if we use the word *"WATER"* the vowels are *"a"* and *"e."* By analogy, if it were a Hebrew word, all they would have had would have been *"WTR."* They knew what the word meant. We would have recognized it, but with other vowels, it might have been *"WAITER."* So, to safeguard the Words of the Hebrew Bible, to be certain what the Words of God were saying and teaching, God put in the vowel markings underneath the consonants from the very beginning. For example, you might find a small *"T"* which is the sound *"ah"*; you might find three dots which is the sound *"eh"*; or you might find two dots which is the sound *"ay"*; one dot is *"ee."*

These are called *matres lectiones,* (*"mothers of reading"*) which enabled Gentiles (and other Jews who were not as familiar with the Words) to read those Hebrew Words with the vowels in there and know exactly what word it would be. So it would be, for instance "*WATER*" instead of "*WAITER.*" These Masoretes guarded the consonantal text and also all of the vowels.

Hebrew Vowels Were Vital

They wanted to make sure we knew what those Words were, especially for the benefit of those of us who are not Jews, and for the Jews who would not understand the Hebrew Words.

The Masoretes flourished from about 500 to 1000 A.D. They were supposed to have standardized the Hebrew Old Testament in about 600-700 A.D. by carefully guarding the vowel pointings which were in the originals. These vowels aid in the pronunciation of the consonantal text. Their text is called the Masoretic Text or "MT" if you want to abbreviate it. Some people spell the word "*Massoretic*," some "*Masoretic*" which I prefer.

4. The Hebrew Words Used by the KING JAMES BIBLE. What about the Hebrew Words used by the KING JAMES BIBLE translators? Here's some background on it.

The Hebrew Words Under the KJB

The Daniel Bomberg edition, 1516-1517, was called the *First Rabbinic Bible.* Then in 1524-25, Bomberg published a second edition edited by Jacob Ben Chayyim (or Ben Hayyim) iben Adonijah. This is called the Ben Chayyim edition of the Hebrew Words. Daniel Bomberg's edition, on which the KING JAMES BIBLE is based was the Ben Chayyim Masoretic Text. This was called the *Second Great Rabbinic Bible.* This became the standard Masoretic text for the next 400 years. These are the Words that underlie the King James Bible.

For four hundred years, those were the Old Testament Hebrew Words that were accepted without question. Nobody translated the Old Testament except by using these Words. [This is from *Biblical Criticism Historical, Literal, Textual* by Harrison, Waltkie and Guthrie, 1978, pages 47-82.]

The 1906 & 1912 Kittel Hebrew

The Ben Chayyim Masoretic Text was used even in the first two editions of *Biblia Hebraica* by Rudolf Kittel. The dates on those first two editions were 1906 and 1912. Kittel used the same Hebrew Words as those used by the King James Bible translators.

The edition that was used when I was a student of Dr. Merrill Frederick Unger at Dallas Theological Seminary (1948-53), was the 1937 edition of the *Biblia Hebraica* by Rudolf Kittel who died in 1929.

Kittel Changed Hebrew in 1937

After Kittel's death, in 1937, the publishers changed his Hebrew edition and followed what they called the Ben Asher Masoretic edition instead of the Ben Chayyim edition. They followed, in that text, the Leningrad Manuscript, (B19a or "L.") The date of this manuscript is given as 1008 A.D. These were not the traditional Masoretic Hebrew Words that had been used for over 400 years (from about 1525 to 1937). These traditional Words were the basis of the King James Bible.

The 1937 edition of Rudolf Kittel's Old Testament Hebrew words followed this Leningrad Manuscript. **This means that even the Hebrew words used as a basis for the NASV, NIV, NKJV and other modern versions are different from the Hebrew Words used for the King James Bible.** In addition to the various changes in the Hebrew text at the top of the page, the footnotes in Rudolf Kittel's *BIBLIA HEBRAICA* suggest about 20,000 to almost 30,000 changes throughout the whole Old Testament.

The reason that most of the Hebrew departments (in colleges, universities, and seminaries who teach Hebrew) use the **Ben Asher Hebrew Text** instead of the **Ben Chayyim Hebrew Text** is the same reason these same people use the critical Greek text in the New Testament. They believe the "oldest" texts, either in Hebrew or in Greek, must always be the best. Not necessarily.

Gnostics Corrupted Vatican & Sinai

I will speak about the New Testament Words later, but I want to summarize some things about those Words here. I believe these so-called "old" texts of the New Testament, such as Manuscripts Vatican ("B") and Sinai ("Aleph") and about forty-three others that follow them, were corrupted by Gnostic heretics within the first 100 years after the original Greek New Testament books were written.

Therefore, even though these manuscripts might be written on the oldest materials, their "*words*" were **doctored** by Gnostic heretics and therefore are not the "*best*." The Words found in other manuscripts, even though they might be found in materials that were later, if they follow the Words of the originals they must, therefore, be the ones to use. Those Words which I believe agree with the original documents are those which the King James Bible has followed.

Then there was a revision of Rudolf Kittel's 1937 *Biblia Hebraica*. It was called the *Biblia Hebraica Stuttgartensia* It was published in Stuttgart, Germany in 1967/77. As in Rudolf Kittel's 1937 edition, it was based on the **Ben Asher words** of the single **Leningrad Codex.** There were approximately the same number of footnotes as in the 1937 Kittel edition which suggested that the Hebrew words in the text should be changed in these 20,000 to about 30,000 different places.

5. Nineteen Erroneous Documents Used to "Correct" the Masoretic Hebrew Words.

19 Suggested Footnote Changes

Not only are the Hebrew words used by the modern versions taken from the questionable *Biblia Hebraica Stuttgartensia* or the *Biblia Hebraica Kittel* (with their 20,000 to 30,000 footnotes suggesting changes in the Hebrew) but the New International Version (NIV) and other modern versions accept these suggested footnote changes and actually make many of these changes in their translations. There are at least nineteen types of such corrections made to the Hebrew words by these English versions which I will identify below.

I will be quoting in part from *ASV, NASV, and NIV Departures from the Traditional Hebrew and Greek Text*, which I wrote some time ago [**BFT #986** @ **$9.00** + **$5.00 S&H**] In this study, I have listed a total of 103 examples of changes from the Hebrew Words and twenty-three Greek examples. I print the Masoretic Hebrew Words with the Bomberg Edition as the basis of the King James Bible. Then we print what the American Standard Version of 1901 has, the New American Standard Version of 1960 has, and what the New International Version of 1969 has. I also show what the King James Bible has. The Masoretic Words and the King James Bible agree with each other, but these other versions depart from the Masoretic Words in these examples. I could have picked from hundreds of other examples. In this study, I list on page A-9, at the bottom, some of the other ways of departing from the Hebrew Words, including the following eleven together with eight more sources listed in the NIV's Preface, pages viii-ix:.

(1) The Septuagint, LXX, the Greek Old Testament. The American Standard Version, New American Standard Version, and the New International Version departed in the Old Testament seventy-three times (35% of the 103 departures I have listed in here) preferring the Septuagint words over the Hebrew Words. That Greek Old Testament is a very deficient translation from the Hebrew Words into the Greek. In many books and places, it is just like the Living Version in looseness. It is a paraphrase, and a **perversion.** In fact, in the beginning of this document [**BFT #986**] I have an analysis of the Septuagint, showing how bad it is as a translation. There are quotations from the *International Standard Bible Encyclopedia* (I.S.B.E.) and comments as to why the Masoretic Words should be followed instead of the Septuagint.

(2) Conjecture, No Reason Given. In sixty-seven examples out of the 103 (32% of the time), the Masoretic Hebrew Words were scuttled merely because of **conjecture.** In other words, these editors don't even have Hebrew Words, Greek words, Latin words, or any other words. They don't have any sources at all. They just say, "*We want it to read this way.*"

Dr. Unger's Isaiah Conjectures

When I was studying Hebrew at Dallas Theological Seminary, (1948-53), as I mentioned before, our teacher was Dr. Merrill Frederick Unger (who wrote *Unger's Bible Dictionary*, etc). We were reading in the book of Isaiah, using the Rudolf Kittel 1937 Hebrew edition (*Biblia Hebraica*). Of course, this edition has from 20,000 to 30,000 footnotes which suggest that the Hebrew Words should be changed in these ways. On occasion, Dr. Unger would read the Hebrew in a way that differed even from the Kittel words. The basis for his alternate reading often came from one of the footnotes. But sometimes, there was no footnote change suggested. It was just Dr. Unger's "*conjecture.*"

On one occasion, as we were translating the book of Isaiah, I raised my hand and said, "*Dr. Unger, why did you change this Word?*" He replied, "*It just reads better that way.*" When the footnotes want to suggest a change and there is no documentation for the change other than "*conjecture,*" the editors put "*L*" in the footnotes. This "*L*" stands for the Latin word, "*legendum,*" meaning "*which read.*" When they are following the Septuagint, or some other version, or the Latin Vulgate, the footnote reads, "*with the Latin Vulgate,*" etc. But sometimes they just have an "*L.*" In fact, in Genesis 1:9, there's an "*L.*" After the "*L,*" it says "*probably this.*" In other words, there's no evidence, no document. It is just conjecture and guesswork. How Bible-believing Christians can allow guesswork and conjecture to determine their Bible is indeed an unwise and unscriptural procedure. .

(3) The Syriac Version. In twenty examples out of the 103 (10% of the time), these editors changed the "*correct*" traditional Masoretic Hebrew Words into words from the Syriac version.

(4) A Few Hebrew Manuscripts. Sometimes, just a "*few*" Hebrew manuscripts were used to "*correct*" the traditional Masoretic Words.

(5) The Latin Vulgate. Sometimes the Latin Vulgate (the Latin translation of the Bible), was used to "*correct*" the traditional Masoretic Hebrew Words.

(6) The Dead Sea Scrolls. In eight examples out of the 103 (4% of the time) the Dead Sea Scrolls were used to "*correct*" the traditional Hebrew Masoretic Words. When Mrs. Waite and I visited Israel in 1982, we went into the Qumran caves where the so-called Dead Sea Scrolls were found. They were preserved by the Essenes. Among other things, they have the book of Isaiah. The guide told us that there was very little difference between the Dead Sea Scrolls and the traditional Hebrew Words of the book of Isaiah. But where the Scrolls differ from the traditional Hebrew Words, their readings should be rejected.

According to tradition, these Essenes fled from Jerusalem to Qumran. They took some of the Hebrew Bible scrolls with them. But, when there is a difference between them, why should we use the Dead Sea Scrolls instead of the traditional Masoretic Words which the Hebrews in Jerusalem had so carefully guarded? We must never do this. These Essenes left the Hebrew synagogue in Jerusalem. They left the Jewish beliefs that their fathers had. They were an offshoot of Judaism and a false, heretical cult.

Two Dead Sea Scroll's Problems

There are at least two reasons for questioning these Dead Sea Scrolls where they might differ with the traditional Masoretic Hebrew Words:

1. They might have had, in some places, corrupt Hebrew Words that they began with;

2. They might have been careless, in some places, in the transmission or copying of these Words.

Both of these matters are unknown, hence, we should never use the wording of the Dead Sea Scrolls to replace the traditional Masoretic Hebrew Words which have been so meticulously preserved.

---

(7) Aquila. Sometimes editors have followed Aquila, a Greek Old Testament translation, to "*correct*" the traditional Masoretic Hebrew Words.

(8) The Samaritan Pentateuch . Sometimes the editors followed the Samaritan Pentateuch to "*correct*" the traditional Masoretic Hebrew Words. This contains the first five books of Moses which the Samaritans used. The Samaritans were a mixed people who had a different translation of the Old Testament.

(9) Quotations from Jerome. Sometimes the editors "*corrected*" the traditional Masoretic Hebrew Words by using quotations from Jerome, who translated the Latin Vulgate.

(10)   Josephus. Sometimes the editors used quotes from Josephus, a Jewish historian, to "*correct*" the traditional Masoretic Hebrew Words.

(11)   An Ancient Hebrew Scribal Tradition. Sometimes editors use an ancient Hebrew scribal tradition to "*correct*" the traditional Masoretic Hebrew Words.

(12)   The *BIBLIA HEBRAICA* of Kittel or Stuttgartensia. Sometimes the editors use false Hebrew words taken from the many suggested "*corrections*" to the traditional Masoretic Hebrew Words that they find in either the *Biblia Hebraica* of Kittel (BHK) or Stuttgartensia (BHS).

(13)   A Variant Hebrew Reading in the Margin. Sometimes editors use these variant Hebrew readings to "correct" the traditional Masoretic Hebrew Words.

(14) Words in the Consonantal Text Divided Differently. Sometimes editors use the Hebrew consonantal words divided differently to "*correct*" the traditional Masoretic Hebrew Words.

(15)   Symmachus. Sometimes editors use this Greek translation of the Old Testament to "*correct*" the traditional Masoretic Hebrew Words.

(16)   Theodotion. Sometimes editors use this Greek translation of the Old Testament to "*correct*" the traditional Masoretic Hebrew Words.

(17)   The Targums. Sometimes editors use Targums (translations of the Hebrew into Aramaic) to "*correct*" the traditional Masoretic Hebrew Words.

(18)   The *Juxta Hebraica* of Jerome for the Psalms. Sometimes editors use the Juxta Hebraica in the Psalms of Jerome to "*correct*" the traditional Masoretic Hebrew Words.

(19)   A Different Set Of Hebrew Vowels. Sometimes editors use a different set of Hebrew vowels to "*correct*" the traditional Masoretic Hebrew Words. We should just leave alone the traditional Masoretic Hebrew Words without any "*correction*" by anything. Leave it alone, and let it be! God has preserved it just as it is.

6. My Conclusion on the Traditional Hebrew Masoretic Words.

Let the Hebrew Words Alone!

My conclusion on the traditional Masoretic Hebrew Words is this: There may be some places in the text of the Daniel Bomberg Hebrew edition of the traditional Masoretic Hebrew Words where there are seeming contradictions. For instance, the king may be eighteen years old or eight years old. Even if there are seeming contradictions, I feel it is imperative to go by the traditional Masoretic Words and let the Lord figure out what may seem like contradictions to us. Keep what God has given and preserved through the ages and let the Lord figure out why. It could be both eight and eighteen and have a harmonization we don't know anything about. The editors of these new versions, have footnotes that depart from the traditional Masoretic Hebrew Words. They often decide the issue on the basis of pure guesswork! But how do you know their decision is the correct one? Just leave the Hebrew text as it is.

The KING JAMES translators came along and saw what the traditional Masoretic Hebrew Words were and simply translated it right over into the English. They didn't quibble about it; they didn't try to harmonize it. For instance, you'll find in Isaiah 9:3 that there is a "*not*" [*LO*] which has been completely eliminated by the new versions. The King James Bible, following the traditional Masoretic Hebrew Words, accurately reads: *"Thou hast multiplied the nation, and **not** increased the joy . . . "* Based on the footnote in the *Biblia Hebraica* of either Kittel or Stuttgart, the following thirteen English versions (by their abbreviations) have omitted the "**not**": NIV, NASV, NKJV, ASV. Darby, ESV, NAB, NJB, NLV, NRS, RSV, RWB, and YLT. These versions have just taken out the "*not*" because they think it makes more sense in their own interpretation. Nevertheless, both the traditional Masoretic Hebrew Words as well as the non-traditional Kittel and Stuttgart editions have [LO] "**not**" right in their texts.

The KJB's Hebrew Words Stand

Never be ashamed of the traditional Masoretic Hebrew text that underlies the KING JAMES BIBLE!! It was accumulated by the Jews in fulfillment of Romans 3:1-2. We agree with Dean John William Burgon who wrote of "*the INCREDIBLE FOLLY OF TINKERING THE HEBREW TEXT.*" [from a letter April 8, 1885, appearing in the *Guardian* as quoted in *JOHN WILLIAM BURGON, LATE DEAN OF CHICHESTER--A BIO-GRAPHY*, 1892, by Edward Mayrick Goulburn, Vol. II, p. 241. [BFT #1619, 801 pages @ $40.00 + $8.00 S&H].

It truly is an "INCREDIBLE FOLLY" for anyone who is guilty of "TINKERING THE HEBREW TEXT." We should leave it alone just as it is!

C.   The Old Testament Traditional Masoretic Hebrew Words Were Authorized by Jesus.
Not only were the Old Testament traditional Masoretic Hebrew Words **accumulated** by Jews (Romans 3:1-2), but they were **authorized** by the Lord Jesus Christ. He authorized the Old Testament traditional Hebrew Words. Here are a few Bible verses that show this.

1. Verses Teaching This Position.

(1) Matthew 4:4. The Lord Jesus Christ was speaking to the devil in the wilderness after He had "*fasted for forty days and forty nights.*" He refuted the devil by using Scripture:

> "*But He answered and said, IT IS WRITTEN, Man shall not live by bread alone, but by EVERY WORD that proceedeth out of the mouth of God.*"

GEGRAPTAI = Bible Preservation

The phrase, *"it is written,"* *(GEGRAPTAI)* is in the Greek perfect tense from the verb, GRAPHO (*"to write"*). What is the meaning of the Greek perfect tense? Whether you refer to Dana and Mantey's *Manual Grammar of the Greek New Testament*, or A. T. Robertson's exhaustive *Greek Grammar* on which it was based, the Greek Perfect tense has a past, present, and future force. The use of the perfect tense for this verb would refer to Old Testament Words that were written in the past, had been preserved in the present time when the Lord Jesus Christ was quoting them, and which Words would continue to be preserved into the future. So, because of the Words used, the Lord Jesus Christ AUTHORIZED the Old Testament He had in His hands.

The first books of the Old Testament were originally written by Moses around 1500 B.C. By using this phrase, *"It is written,"* the Lord Jesus Christ was stating that the Old Testament traditional Hebrew Words were preserved for 1,500 years up to His own times. This means that the **Words of God** have been written down in the past and these very **Words** have been preserved down to the present time when the Lord Jesus Christ used them, and they stand written now in our times in the same way as when they were first written. This is the very essence of Bible Preservation!

(2) Matthew 5:17-18. In this passage, the Lord Jesus Christ spoke about *"the law, or the prophets."* This is a technical term referring to the Old Testament traditional Masoretic Hebrew Words.

The Old Testament's Three Parts

There are three divisions in the Old Testament: the Law, the Prophets, and the Writings. Sometimes the expression, *"the law and the prophets,"* refers to all three divisions (used in Matthew 7:12; 22:40; Luke 16:16; John 1:45; Acts 13:15; and Romans 3:21).

Luke 24:44 mentions the Lord Jesus Christ's reference to all three of these divisions:

> *"And He said unto them, These are the words which I spake unto you, while I was yet with you, that all things must be fulfilled,*

which were written in the law of Moses, and in the prophets, and in the psalms, concerning me."

The Law (the *torah*) refers to the first five books; the Prophets (the *naviim*) refers to both the former and the latter Prophets; and the Writings (the *kethuvim*) refers to the Psalms and the rest of the Old Testament books. Here in Matthew 5, verses 17 and 18 the Lord Jesus Christ said,

"(17) *Think not that I am come to destroy the LAW, or the PRO-PHETS: . . .* (18) *For verily I say unto you, Till heaven and earth pass, one jot or one tittle shall in no wise pass from the Law, till all be fulfilled.*"

By using the words "*one jot or one tittle,*" He referred to Hebrew letters and parts of the letters found in the Old Testament traditional Masoretic Hebrew Words that He possessed in His day. I believe He spoke of "*the law, or the prophets*" using the word, "*law*" to refer to the total Old Testament traditional Masoretic Hebrew Words.

If this be true, the Lord Jesus Christ was stating clearly that until "*all*" of the entire Old Testament traditional Masoretic Hebrew Words were "*fulfilled*" (and these Words have not all been "*fulfilled*"), "*one jot or one tittle shall in no wise pass from the law.*" This would hold true also until "*heaven and earth pass.*" Neither of these things have been accomplished:

1. The entire Old Testament traditional Masoretic Hebrew Words have not been "*fulfilled*"; and

2. "*Heaven and earth*"' have not passed away. Therefore, most clearly, this means that not "*one jot or one tittle*" would be eliminated, effaced, or changed in the slightest manner until "*all be fulfilled.*"

A few more things must be made clear. "*What does "in no wise" mean?*" The Greek words for this are **OU ME**. This combination is the strongest negative expression that exists in the Greek language. A second question should also be asked, "*What is a 'jot' and what is a 'tittle'?*"

Preserved O.T. Letters & Vowels

A "*jot*" represents the smallest letter in the Hebrew alphabet, a "*yodh.*" It looks like our English comma or like our English single quotation mark. The "*tittle*" is the smallest Hebrew accent. It refers to the "*hiriq*" which looks like our English period or dot.

The result of these two verses is that the Lord Jesus Christ put His **authorization** on the Old Testament traditional Masoretic Hebrew Words that

He had in His day–down to the very letters and accents!

(3) Luke 24:27. When the Lord Jesus Christ talked to the disciples on the road to Emmaus, He taught them:

"And beginning at Moses and all the prophets, He expounded unto them the things concerning Himself."

Here is the phrase *"Moses and all the prophets."* It leaves off the *"writings,"* but again, this was referring to the threefold division of the Hebrew Bible: the Law, the Prophets and the Writings. That is an authorization by the Lord Jesus Christ of the Old Testament traditional Masoretic Hebrew Words that were present in His day.

(4) Luke 24:44.

*"And He said unto them, These are the words which I spake unto you, while I was yet with you, that all things must be fulfilled, which were **written** in THE LAW of Moses, and in THE PROPHETS, and in THE PSALMS, concerning Me."*

Greek Perfect Tense Preservation

The Greek word for *"written"* is GEGRAMMENA from GRAPHO. It is a perfect participle. As mentioned in Matthew 4:4 above, the Greek perfect tense indicates something that was written down in the past, has been continuously preserved to the present, and will be continuously preserved into the future.

Christ Quoted Hebrew, Not LXX

The phrase, *"in the Psalms,"* makes it a reference to the complete threefold division of the Hebrew canon:

1. the law of Moses (Torah);

2. the prophets (Naviim); and

3. the Psalms or Writings (Kethuvim).

It is called the *"TANACH"* today by the Jews, taking the *"TA"* for *"TORAH,"* the *"NA"* from *"NAVIIM,"* and the *"CH"* for *"KETHUVIM."* This is the one abbreviation for the entire Masoretic Hebrew Old Testament.

In making reference to these three divisions of the Old Testament, **The Lord Jesus Christ put His hand on the Words of the entire traditional Masoretic Hebrew Old Testament text that existed then and AUTHORIZED it.**

Christ Did Not Quote From the LXX

Many people may ask, "Didn't the Lord Jesus Christ use the Septuagint Version of the Old Testament? Wasn't He referring to that?" No, He was not. He referred to the Law of Moses, the Prophets, and the Psalms (or Writings). In the first place, there was no Septuagint until the late 200's A.D. and was not in existence when the Lord Jesus Christ was on earth. In the second place, even if He were referring to the Septuagint, it does not have that division at all. In fact, aside from the Apocrypha contained in the Septuagint, the order is the same as in our English Bibles, that is, LAW, PSALMS, and PROPHETS instead of, as the Hebrew, LAW, PROPHETS & PSALMS.

As you can see, the Septuagint has the order of books much as we have in our Bibles today. The Hebrew does not have the same order; it ends with the book of 2 Chronicles.

2. Quotations Explaining This Position.

Christ appealed unreservedly to the traditional Masoretic Hebrew Words.

(1) A Quotation from Dr. Edward Hills. Here is a quotation from Dr. Edward Hills, who has written extensively on the subject of the Bible.

> "During His earthly life, the Lord Jesus appealed unreservedly to the very words of the Old Testament text (Matthew 22:42, John 10:34-36), thus indicating His confidence that this text had been accurately transmitted. Not only so, but He also expressed this conviction in the strongest possible manner, `. . . till heaven and earth pass, one jot or one tittle shall in no wise pass from the law till all be fulfilled,' (Matthew 5:18.) . . . Here our Lord Jesus assures us that the Old Testament in common use among the Jews during His earthly ministry was an **ABSOLUTELY TRUSTWORTHY REPRODUCTION OF THE ORIGINAL TEXT WRITTEN BY MOSES AND OTHER . . . WRITERS.**" [BELIEVING BIBLE

STUDY, by Dr. Edward Hills, pp. 5-6].

Christ Never Doubted O.T. Hebrew

The Lord Jesus Christ never refuted any text, any Word, or any letter in the traditional Masoretic Hebrew Old Testament. He did not say, *"Now Moses was misquoted here, it should have been this."* He offered no textual criticism whatever. Had there been any changes, I'm sure He would have corrected it, but He didn't. It stands written (GEGRAPTAI)! His stamp of approval is on the traditional Masoretic Hebrew Words. It was AUTHORIZED by Jesus. He did not authorize the Septuagint, the Latin Vulgate, some scribal tradition, Josephus, Jerome, the Syriac version, or any other document!

(2) A Quotation from Dr. Robert Dick Wilson.

Here is a quotation from Dr. Robert Dick Wilson, who was a conservative Presbyterian, and a teacher there at Princeton Theological Seminary before the flood of Modernism came in. Henry Corey reflected on the life of Dr. Robert Dick Wilson, a man who had mastered some forty-five languages and dialects and who was a staunch defender of the doctrine of verbal inspiration of Scripture. Corey affirmed that Wilson accepted as **accurate** the Masoretic Hebrew text. Corey, quoting Wilson, wrote:

> *"The results of those 30 years' study* [that is what Wilson wrote of his own study of Scripture in the Hebrew] *which I have given to the text has been this: I can affirm that there's not a page of the Old Testament in which we need have any doubt. We can be absolutely certain that substantially we have the text of the Old Testament that Christ and the Apostles had and which was in existence from the beginning." [WHICH BIBLE, 1st edition, by Dr. David Otis Fuller, pp. 80-81].*

Here is a man who studied, and studied, and found the traditional Masoretic Hebrew Words to be accurate and solid. So I see no reason why we should have any other foundation for the Old Testament than the traditional Masoretic Hebrew Words that underlie the King James Bible. It is the **Daniel Bomberg edition**, edited by **Ben Chayyim**–the **2nd Rabbinic Bible of 1524-25**.

3. The Alternative to Believing This

Position. You might say, "*What is the alternative? What if you do not accept the **Daniel Bomberg edition** of the **traditional Masoretic Hebrew Words** on which the King James Bible is based as the **authoritative** Hebrew text from which to translate?*"

The alternative, quite logically, would be to accept some other base from which to translate the Old Testament. What other base are you going to use? Are you going to use the Kittel *Biblia Hebraica* (**BHK**) which was based upon the same text as the King James Bible in 1906 and 1912, and then was revised and scrapped for another Hebrew text in 1937? Or are you going to use the 1967/77 *Biblia Hebraica Stuttgartensia* (**BHS**) which is a revised Kittel?

The Vital Choice of O.T. Hebrew

If you're going to use the base that is printed in the defective Hebrew words at the top of the page in either BHK or BHS, are you going to use also some or all of the changes in these words suggested in the footnotes-- 20,000 to 30,000 of them? If so, which ones are you going to use? Are you going to use only the ones they used in the New King James Version? Are you going to use only the ones they used in the New American Standard Version? Are you going to use only the ones they used in the New International Version? Are you going to use 25% of them? 50% of them? Or are you going to use all of them?

Or are you going to become a doubter, thinking that we don't really know what the Old Testament is? Are you going to take the position that "*We can't be certain of the Hebrew Old Testament, so we must doubt all of it*"? **Satan is the master of deceitful doubting and he is the author of all this confusion.** Once you forsake a standard, you are adrift in a sea of doubts. There's nothing to take its place. Young Christians and people in the pews who have not been saved too many years might say, "*If there's all this bickering and fighting among the theologians and pastors as to the right Hebrew Old Testament text to use, I give up and throw up my hands.*" The devil wins if he can plant the seeds of confusion and doubts into the hearts of men and women as well as boys and girls.

My Position on the O.T. Hebrew

After much study, thinking, and praying about this subject, I have personally arrived at a strong conviction on the traditional Masoretic Hebrew Words. I will not budge from the traditional Masoretic Hebrew Words which underlie the King James Bible. That is it. Personally, I am not going to move from this base. I don't want to change anything. We're going to stand right there. Somebody must stand.

Martin Luther said, "Here I stand; I can do no other." He wasn't going to move from salvation by faith (*sola fide*), salvation by grace (*sola gratia*), salvation only by the Scripture (*sola scriptura*), and only through the Lord Jesus Christ (*sola Christi*). He wasn't going to follow the Pope. He wasn't going to follow the decrees of the Church Councils. He was standing on the Words of God alone! Though we might not be Lutherans like Martin Luther, and though we might not agree with many of his beliefs and practices, we must not budge on these four things, including especially on the Words of the Bible. If we do budge on these, we are like a wave of the sea, driven by the wind and tossed.

4. Illustration of Rejecting This Position.

Let me point out an illustration about the Old Testament traditional Masoretic Words.

Changing the O.T. Hebrew Words

The NIV Interlinear Hebrew-English Old Testament (1979) has four volumes. It is edited by John R. Kohlenberger, III, and published by Zondervan. Zondervan is supposed to be a Bible-believing, evangelical publishing house, although I do not agree with many of the books they publish. I want to show you what they have done to the Old Testament text. Rudolf Kittel, who wrote this *Biblia Hebraica*, the two editions earlier and then the edition of 1937, was an apostate German rationalist.

Kittel was a believer in the Graf-Welhausen documentary hypothesis of the Pentateuch. It is called the JEDP theory. He did not believe in the inerrancy of Scripture. Theologically, he was all that he shouldn't be. This man, although we don't believe in the Hebrew text he used (he used the **Ben**

Asher instead of the **Ben Chayyim** text), at least put the Hebrew text on the top of the page. He kept the changes separate and distinct by putting them in the footnotes, so you could read his Masoretic text as it was. The same method was followed later in the *Biblia Hebraica Stuttgartensia.*

NIV's Changing the Hebrew Words

What did the NIV and Zondervan do, though? Any time they wanted to change the Masoretic Hebrew text, they put it right up in the text, instead of in the footnotes. Let me illustrate: Genesis 4:8 says in the King James Bible and in the Hebrew Masoretic Text:

> *"And Cain talked with Abel his brother: and it came to pass, when they were in the field, that Cain rose up against Abel his brother, and slew him."*

In the NIV it says,

> *"Cain said to Abel, his brother, '_Let us go out to the field_. . .'"*

There's nothing in the Hebrew text to justify these words above that are **bold** and underlined. All the other Hebrew versions leave it out, but Kohlenberger puts it right into the text. He has a footnote on it in very small type which says,

> *"This Hebrew reading and translation is **conjectured** on the basis of the early versions listed above in Note 1."*

The Dangers of Hebrew Conjecture

So they conjecture it and put into Hebrew what is nowhere found in any Hebrew manuscript. A devout Jew would never do such a thing! All these unbelievers, like Kittel and the German Stuttgart editors, at least put any suggested changes from the Hebrew text into the footnotes. But Kohlenberger and Zondervan, who are supposed to be believers in Christ, put the conjecture right into the Hebrew text. It is a sad day when an alleged and supposedly Bible-believing evangelical will emend the traditional Masoretic Hebrew Words themselves.

As I've pointed out before, the Old Testament basis of our King James Bible are the traditional Masoretic Hebrew Words. They are the Words of the **2nd Rabbinic Bible, Daniel Bomberg Edition, edited by Ben Chayyim** in

1524-25.

The 400-Year Hebrew Record

The date of the 1st Bomberg Edition was 1516-1517. It was called the First Rabbinic Bible. During this time they came up with standard traditional Masoretic Hebrew Old Testament Words which lasted without question for over 400 years.

That standard was used even in Kittel's first two editions, 1906 and 1912. Let us stick to this standard firmly!

II. THE KING JAMES BIBLE IS GOD'S WORDS KEPT INTACT IN ENGLISH BECAUSE OF ITS SUPERIOR NEW TESTAMENT GREEK WORDS

I believe the King James Bible is based on **superior** New Testament Greek Words. I believe this for two reasons:

1. The first reason is that the *Textus Receptus* that underlies the King James Bible was **accepted by the churches**.

2. The second reason is that the *Textus Receptus* that underlies the King James Bible is **attested by the evidence**.

Before taking up these two main topics, let us look at a little background information.

A. The Chief Opponent of the *Textus Receptus* Today. The New Testament Greek

The New Testament Greek words which are used today in most colleges, universities, and seminaries (even conservative and/or fundamental ones) are those found in the Gnostic Greek critical texts either of the United Bible Societies (UBS) 3rd or 4th editions, or the *Nestle/Aland Greek New Testament,* 26th or 27th editions.

History of the False Greek N.T.

As of this writing, this text has gone through twenty-seven editions thus far. Nestle began his critical Greek edition in 1898, following the basic text of Bishop Westcott and Professor Hort and three other editions of his day. The Greek-English edition I have is dated 1981. I believe the 27th Greek edition came out in 1993. From 1898 to 1993, is about ninety-five years. If you divide ninety-five by twenty-seven, you can see that they have come out, on the average, with one new, updated, changed, different edition of the Greek New Testament every 3.5 years!

What does that tell you as to the uncertainty these editors have in **God's preservation** of His New Testament Words? It tells you that these men really are not certain about what the Greek New Testament Words are. The Nestle/Aland words are about the same words as Bishop Westcott and Professor Hort included in their 1881 edition, with a few changes here and there. Both words of both of these editions are based for the most part on the Gnostic Vatican and Sinai Greek manuscripts of Alexandria, Egypt. The edition of *Nestle/Aland Greek New Testament 27th Edition* that I have has with it, in parallel columns, the English of the Revised Standard Version, which is copyrighted by the apostate-led National Council of Churches.

B. The Editors of the *Nestle/Aland* Greek Words.

This *Nestle/Aland* Greek text was named for Eberhard Nestle, a German, and Kurt Aland, his grandson who was also a German. It was made up by a committee consisting of Kurt Aland (an unbeliever), Matthew Black (an unbeliever), Carlo M. Martini (a cardinal of the Roman Catholic Church), Bruce Metzger (from Princeton, a man who demonstrated his apostasy as editor of the *Reader's Digest Bible*), and Alan Wigren (from Chicago, an apostate also). All these were editors of the 27th edition of the *Nestle/Aland* Greek New Testament words.

C. These Words Underlie the Modern English Versions.

These Greek New Testament words, or those like them, are the basic words that underlie the modern versions such as: the English Revised Version (ERV) of 1881, the American Standard Version (ASV) of 1901, the New American Standard Version (NASV) of 1960, the New International Version (NIV) of 1969, the New English Version (NEV) of 1961, the English Standard Version (ESV) of 2001, and most of the other modern versions.

Gnostic Greek Words Used Today

These New Testament Gnostic Greek words are what the so-called scholarly world as well as New Evangelicals and many Fundamentalists (sad to say) are using.

The fact that there have been TWENTY-SEVEN EDITIONS IN NINETY-FIVE YEARS (a new edition every 3.5 years) would give you the distinct impression that these men, and their followers, who put confidence in the words of their Greek editions, have no assurance whatsoever of what are and what are not the very and the exact Greek Words of God in the New Testament! I certainly wouldn't want to be in their shoes!

Confidence in the KJB's Greek

I have confidence in the Words of the *Received Text* that underlie the King James Bible. I also have confidence in the King James Bible as the most accurate English translation of that text. For this reason, I believe that the words of the King James Bible are the Words of God in English!

D. The Greek Words That Underlie the
KING JAMES BIBLE. The King James Bible's New

Testament was based on Words from the traditional Greek text. It has been printed both by the Trinitarian Bible Society (BFT #471 @ $14.00 + $5.00 S&H) and the Dean Burgon Society (BFT #1670 @ $35.00 + $5.00 S&H). The Dean Burgon Society's text is a photographic reproduction of the 1894 edition of Dr. Frederick H. A. Scrivener, including both the Words and the footnotes in large print. The Trinitarian Bible Society's edition has only the Words, but not the footnotes and Appendix. It is in smaller print. The Scrivener Greek Text was published by the Cambridge University Press.

The Sound KJB's Greek Words

This *Textus Receptus* which underlies the King James Bible's New Testament, was basically Beza's 5th edition of 1598. Dr. Frederick H. A. Scrivener, in his *New Testament in Greek According to the Text Followed in the Authorised Version Together with the Variations Adopted in the Revised Version* of 1881, lists about 190 places where Scrivener thought the KJB editors departed from Beza's 5th edition in favor of eight other sources (Cf. pp. 648-656 of BFT #1670] These Greek Words are the exact Words that underlie the King James Bible.

The Changeless KJB Greek Words

These Words haven't changed. These Words haven't been revised since 1611. I don't believe these Words need any revising. These Greek Words are the only Words that should be used to translate the New Testament into the languages of the world.

These are the Words I want to talk about. Though there are other *Traditional Received Texts*, I believe that Scrivener's is the most accurate. The family of the Traditional Received Texts have been handed down from generation to generation by the church.

E. The Words of the *Textus Receptus* Family Have Been Accepted by the Churches.

There are various editions in the family called the *Textus Receptus*. I am combining them all together and referring to them as members of one textual family. This family I call the "*Textus Receptus*." As I have said before, I believe the *Textus Receptus* Words underlying the King James Bible are the most refined and the best. I believe and accept these Words as the original verbal plenary preserved New Testament Greek Words.

Why the KJB's Greek Is Superior

There are two reasons why I believe that the family known as the *Textus Receptus* or *Received Text* is superior:

1. First, this text has been accepted by the churches. It is traditional. It has been handed down by the people who knew what they were talking about.

2. Second, this text has been attested by the evidence. There is evidence that this is a superior text. We don't have to take it only by faith. There is strong evidence to indicate that this is the text that should be used, and that it is historic.

37 Historical TR Links

I will be giving a total of thirty-seven links in the historical chain of evidence in favor of this *Textus Receptus* family. I will show how, through the history of the Christian church, various churches, groups, organizations, and documents have accepted this text, the *Textus Receptus*, as the true Greek text which we should accept as our New Testament and from which we should do all of our New Testament translations. I believe that these Greek words go all the way back to the original manuscripts of the Greek New Testament. They have been accepted ever since they were written down.

F. Westcott and Hort Refused to Accept the *Textus Receptus* Greek.

Though there was some scattered opposition to the *Textus Receptus* (TR) in years before, the **concerted** effort against the *Textus Receptus* came in 1881 and after. In 1881, two theological heretics (**posing as conservatives**) from the Anglican Church (Church of England), Bishop Westcott and Professor Hort, published their Greek text that rejected the *Textus Receptus*.

Over 8,000 Greek Text Differences

I once counted 5,604 places or sections (including the twelve verses in both Mark 16:9-20 and John 7:53-8:11) in the Greek New Testament of Dr. Scrivener where the English Revised Version and the Westcott and Hort Greek text altered in some way the *Textus Receptus*. Dr. Jack Moorman has produced a book comparing the Scrivener *Textus Receptus* that underlies the King James Bible with the Nestle/Aland critical Greek text that underlies the New International Version (NIV) and other modern versions. He found over 8,000 differences between these two Greek texts. It is called *8,000 Differences between the Textus Receptus and the Critical Text* (BFT #3084 @ $20.00 + $5.00 S&H).

Westcott was a bishop of the Anglican Church; Hort was a professor at Cambridge University. I've written a little booklet entitled, *The Theological Heresies Of Westcott And Hort* [BFT #595 @ $7.00 + $3.00 S&H] In this study, I used about 125 quotations from five of their books to show that they are **apostates, liberals, and unbelievers.** And yet, they are the ones that altered the Greek New Testament Words in over 8,000 places. Professor Hort wrote an *INTRODUCTION* to this revolutionary Westcott and Hort Greek text. **If we don't understand the part of Westcott and Hort in this, we won't understand why there was the change from the *Textus Receptus* to the new Westcott and Hort type of text.**

Why did this Greek text originate? It was because Professor Hort (in conjunction with Bishop Westcott) propounded a totally erroneous theory. This theory was found in his *INTRODUCTION* to that text. It was written in 1882 and contained 530 pages. Our Bible For Today ministry has reprinted this *INTRODUCTION* so that people who are interested in it can see what Hort wrote, including his contradictions and falsehoods [BFT #1303 @ $25.00 + $5.00 S&H].

Bob Jones Univ. & Gnostic Greek

Professor Hort's writing in that book swayed the whole scholarly world both on his side of the Atlantic Ocean (including England, Scotland, and Germany), as well as on this side of the Atlantic. This included B. B. Warfield at Princeton Theological Seminary, and other Presbyterian schools, Baptist institutions, such as A. T. Robertson's Southern Baptist Seminary at Louisville, and many others. For instance, Dr. Brokenshire (who was trained by B. B. Warfield and others at Princeton Seminary) brought this false critical text to Fundamentalist Bob Jones University in the 1950's and it has been there ever since. These institutions just threw out the New Testament Greek Words that had been in the hands of people since the apostolic age. In 1881, Westcott and Hort published a new Greek text, changing the *Received Text* in over 8,000 places. This was the text that had been used in the Church from the beginning of the writing of the New Testament.

G. The Westcott and Hort Critical Text Has Over 8,000 Differences With The *Textus Receptus.*

As I mentioned above, Dr. Jack Moorman has produced a book comparing the Scrivener *Textus Receptus* that underlies the King James Bible with the Nestle/Aland critical Greek text that underlies the New International Version (NIV) and other modern versions. He found over 8,000 differences between these two Greek texts. The over 8,000 "**differences**" between the two Greek texts can be either additions, subtractions, or changes in other ways. It is called *8,000 Differences between the Textus Receptus and the Critical Text* (**BFT #3084** @ **$20.00 + $5.00 S&H**). It was published by both the Bible For Today, Incorporated and the Dean Burgon Society, Incorporated in 2006.

Before this, in December, 1988, Dr. Moorman also wrote a book entitled: *MISSING IN MODERN BIBLES--IS THE FULL STORY BEING TOLD?* [**BFT #1726** @ **$8.00 + $4.00 S&H**]. It was published by The Bible For Today in April, 1989.

2,886 Shorter Gnostic Greek Words

In preparation for this book, Dr. Moorman counted every word of the *Textus Receptus Greek* and also every word of the *Nestle/Aland Greek Text.* On a chapter by chapter count, he came up with the fact that the *Nestle/Aland* was SHORTER than the *Textus Receptus* by 2,886 words. According to some counts, this is 934 words more than were omitted from the Westcott and Hort text. (1,952 vs. 2,886). The omitting of 2,886 Greek words is the equivalent, in number of English words involved (if they were put together one word after the other), of DROPPING OUT THE ENTIRE BOOKS OF 1 PETER AND 2 PETER! Pastor Moorman's book is eighty large pages. [BFT #1726 @ $8.00 + $4.00 S&H]

Some Fundamental leaders have said that these 8,000 differences don't make any really difference in any translations because there are no doctrines involved. This is entirely false. Dr. Jack Moorman has also written a book called *Early Manuscripts, Church Fathers, and the Authorized Version* (**BFT #3230** @ **$20.00 + $5.00 S&H**). It was published in 2005 by the Bible For Today, Incorporated. On pages 119-312, Dr. Moorman lists over 356 doctrinal passages that are involved in these 8,000 differences between these two Greek texts. I have listed over 158 of these 356 doctrinal passages in Chapter V of my book, *Defending the King James Bible* (BFT #1594 @ $12.00 + $4.00 S&H).

---

356 Gnostic Doctrinal Passages

If this is true, and it is, that there are over 356 doctrinal passages found in the critical Greek text of Nestle/Aland (NA) 26th and 27th and the United Bible Societies (UBS), this makes many doctrinal differences in all of the various language versions based upon these critical Gnostic Greek texts, including most of the English versions. The reason for this is that these translations have been based upon either the NA or the UBS Greek texts. This includes the English versions of the ERV, ASV, NASV, RSV, NRSV, ESV, NEV, and many others.

H. These Two Greek Texts Have Ir-reconcilable Differences. The foundational New

Testament and Old Testament texts in question are fundamentally and irreconcilably different. It is impossible that they can come up with anything but **confusion.** Talk about doctrinal changes! In my booklet *The Case For the Received Text of Hebrew and Greek Underlying the King James Version-- A Summary Of the Evidence & Argument* [BFT #83 @$7.00 + $3.00 S&H]. I analyzed three books that summed up the argument and put it as clearly as I could in 1971. This is available from the Bible For Today. In the back of this **BFT #83,** "*The Case for the King James Version of the Bible*, page thirty-nine, I have listed some very important verses, Greek texts, and English translations that eliminate parts of them, using forty-four different versions of the New Testament. There are 162 key verses to compare in these Greek texts. In each of these translations you have a number of verses, or parts of verses, that are omitted. For instance, the Revised Standard Version omits some or all of 158 of the 162 test verses, or 97%; Nestle's Greek text omits some or all of 155 of the 162 test verses, or 96%. You can look at the other forty-two editions or versions rate as to these 162 test verses.

I. Many Doctrinal Differences in the Two Greek Texts.

As I have written above, in Chapter V of my book, *Defending the King James Bible* (BFT #1594 @ $12.00 + $4.00 S&H), I have listed 158 passages where doctrines are involved in Bible versions that Bible-believing Christians are using today. These four versions are the NASV, the NIV, the footnotes in the study edition of the NKJV and the New Berkeley version.

In my booklet, *The Case For the Received Text of Hebrew and Greek Underlying the King James Version-- A Summary Of the Evidence & Argument* [BFT #83 @$7.00 + $3.00 S&H], I took these 162 key verses, listed them, and then classified them as to doctrines that are omitted or changed.

Among these doctrines that are changed include:

1. the deity of Christ (sixteen verses on this);
2. the omission of the Lord Jesus Christ's full title;
3. the virgin birth of Christ;
4. the omission of "*begotten*" which alters His eternal Sonship and His relationship with the Father;
5. the omission of "Alpha and Omega" involving Christ's eternal generation and eternal future;
6. the omission of Christ's omnipresence;
7. the omission of Christ's eternal future state;
8. the omission of Christ's part in the creation of the world;
9. the omission of the fact that salvation is only through genuine faith in the Lord Jesus Christ;
10. the weakening of the fact of Christ's bodily resurrection;
11. the weakening of Christ's bodily ascension;
12. the weakening of Christ's bodily coming again;
13. weakening of Christ's great commission.
14. Here is what the argument is. Fundamental church leaders, teachers in schools, and authors in their books have falsely said repeatedly something to this effect:

"*The Westcott and Hort text (or the Nestle/Aland or the United Bible Societies or any other critical Greek text) have **very few textual differences** with the Textus Receptus and there are **no doctrines involved** in any of these differences.*"

Both of these statements are woefully false. Over 356 doctrinal passages are involved in almost 100% of the modern English versions that are printed today.

J.   The Early Gnostic Heretics Polluted the Westcott-and-Hort-type Text.

Gnostic Corruption of Greek Words

Do you know why the Gnostic heretics took out some things but not all of them? They wanted the Bible to agree with their false doctrines. These Gnostic heretics, who flourished in the first hundred years after the Bible was written, did not have every New Testament book in their possession. For this reason, they couldn't rip out, change, recopy, add, or forge various verses throughout the New Testament. They could do only such things with the books they had in their hands. So some books escaped the Gnostic heretics' knives. But, if you take out anything or add anything, you have a defective Bible. How many Words of God have to be left out of your Bible before it is no longer 100% God's Words? Just one? That would be enough for me. But when you have over 8,000 differences involving over 356 doctrinal passages, you have a serious problem.

K. Why the NIV & NASV and Others Are Not the Words of God in English. Can I hold up the New International Version and say it is a translation of the Words of God in English? No, I can't because there are over 8,000 reasons why it isn't the Words of God in English. Can I hold up the New American Standard Version and say it is a translation of the Words of God in English? No, I can't. Can I even hold up the New King James Bible and say it is a translation of the Words of God in English? No, I can't.

KJB–the Words of God in English

Can I hold up the KING JAMES VERSION and say it is the accurate translation of the Words of God in English? Yes. All the words are there, accurately translated by master translators.

L. This Writer Was Trained in the Westcott and Hort Camp.

The Case for the King James Version [**BFT #83** @ **$7.00** + **$4.00 S&H**] was the first booklet I wrote on the subject of the superiority of the King James Bible. It was written in 1971.

Trained in Gnostic Greek Words

I was trained to prefer and accept the Westcott and Hort Greek text (now called the *Nestle/Aland* text and the United Bible Societies text) at Dallas Theological Seminary, Dallas, Texas. I was a student there from 1948 through 1953. I received the Master of Theology (Th.M.) and the Doctor of Theology (Th.D.) degrees from that school.

The *Textus Receptus* or the *Received Text* had been, almost without question, the text in use up until 1881, when this change took place. For almost 1,800 years the church had accepted the *Received Text*. Suddenly, many people threw it out.

1,800 Years of Trust–Gone!

Something that had lasted for 1,800 years is now, all of a sudden, branded as being no good, and even worthless. In the days in which we live, you are looked down on and almost thought of as an ignoramus if you stand for the *Textus Receptus* for which Christians and Christian churches down through the centuries have stood. If you don't use the Nestle/Aland Greek text, the United Bible Societies Greek text, or some other critical Greek text, many think something must be wrong with you.

This is a serious situation. This is one of the reasons that two other men and I started the Dean Burgon Society (DBS). I have been the President of the DBS since its beginning in 1978. This is also one of the reasons that I began the Bible For Today ministry in 1971. These two organizations, and others, have been seeking to put the truth of this issue before the people and to defend the traditional *Textus Receptus* Greek Words and the traditional Masoretic Hebrew Words that underlie the King James Bible.

M. The Thirty-Seven Historical Evidences Supporting the Traditional *Textus Receptus* Kind of Greek Words. Here are

the thirty-seven links in the chain of historical evidence to support the *Received* type of Words.

1. Historical Evidences for the Traditional *Textus Receptus* Kind of Words During the Apostolic Age (33–100 A.D.)

1. All of the Apostolic Churches used the Textus Receptus Kind of Words.
2. The churches in Palestine used the Textus Receptus Kind of Words.
3. The Syrian Church at Antioch used the Textus Receptus Kind of Words.

2. Historical Evidences for the Traditional *Textus Receptus* Kind of Words During the Early Church Period (100–312 A.D.).

Gnostic Heresies in 1ˢᵗ 100 Years

Dr. Scrivener and Dean Burgon both agree that, during the first 100 years after the New Testament was written, the greatest corruptions took place to the *Received Text* used by the early church. Those corruptions were made in large part by the Gnostics whose headquarters were in Alexandria, Egypt.

The Vatican ("B") and Sinai (Aleph) manuscripts and the approximately forty-three allies which underlie the Westcott-and-Hort-type text were, I believe, the result of such corruptions. These two manuscripts were from Alexandria, Egypt where these Gnostics were based. Some of these Gnostic heretics which operated in this early period were Marcion, (160 A. D.); Valentinus, (about 160 A. D.); Cyrinthus, (50-100 A. D.); Sabellius, (about 260 A. D.); and many others.

4. The Peshitta Syriac Version, (150 A. D., the second century.) used the Textus Receptus Kind of Words.
5. Papyrus #66 used the Textus Receptus Kind of Words.
6. The Italic Church in Northern Italy (157 A. D.) used the Textus Receptus Kind of Words.
7. The Gallic Church of Southern France (177 A. D.) used the Textus Receptus Kind of Words.
8. The Celtic Church in Great Britain used the Textus Receptus Kind of Words.

Early Churches Used the T.R.

Why did all these early churches have their Bibles based on the traditional *Textus Receptus*?--the churches in Italy, France, and Great Britain--why? Because those were the true Words of God, and they knew it. That was the traditional *Received Text.* They lived in 150 A. D. The Bible was completed in 90-100 A. D. They had the originals right there in their hands and they based their translations on the Greek Words which were pure, accurate, and preserved by God and by the Lord Jesus Christ Who preserves everything.

These churches used these Words of the traditional *Textus Receptus* and not any other. The Gnostic heretics made most of the changes in the Traditional *Textus Receptus* during this time.

Gnostic Heresies in 1st 100 Years

The greatest proportion of these Gnostic heresies, according to both Dr. Scrivener and Dean Burgon, were made during the first 100 years after the completion of the New Testament.

---

9. Church of Scotland and Ireland used the Textus Receptus Kind of Words.
10. The Pre-Waldensian churches used the Textus Receptus Kind of Words.
11. The Waldensians (120 A. D. and onward) used the Textus Receptus Kind of Words.

3. Historical Evidences for the Traditional *Textus Receptus* Kind of Words During the Byzantine Period (312--1453 A.D.)

12. The Gothic Version of the 4th century used the Textus Receptus Kind of Words.

13. Codex W of Matthew in the 4th or 5th century used the Textus Receptus Kind of Words.

14. Codex A in the Gospels (in the 5th century) used the Textus Receptus Kind of Words.

15. The vast majority of extant New Testament manuscripts all used the Textus Receptus Kind of Words.

According to Dr. Jack Moorman in his book, *Forever Settled* (BFT #1428 @ $20.00 + $5.00 S&H) this includes over 99% of the 5,255 manuscripts in existence as of 1967. Though there have been about 300 more found since 1967, it is a safe assumption that this 99% percentage would remain the same.

16. The Greek Orthodox Church used the Textus Receptus Kind of Words.

I don't agree with most of the doctrines and/or practices of the Greek Orthodox Church, but that entire church for over 1,000 years has used the *Textus Receptus* kind of Words. Why? They know the Greek language. They're Greeks. Even though they are modern Greeks, they use the New Testament Words that are based upon the *Textus Receptus* because they are the Words of God, and they know it.

17. The present Greek Church still uses the Textus Receptus Kind of Words.

When Mrs. Waite and I were in Israel, we visited the church which is supposed to be built on the place where Jesus was born. It is called the Church of the Nativity. The Greek Orthodox Church has erected a large Church on that site. It doesn't look anything like the original place of our Lord's birth. I don't even think it is on the proper place. They have commercialized it. In Jerusalem, various groups believe that the Lord Jesus Christ was born in different places, crucified in different places, and buried in different places.

Greek Orthodox Text Uses the T.R.

In the Church of the Nativity, Christ's supposed birth place, we met a Greek Orthodox priest. I said to him, *"You're a member of the Greek Orthodox clergy, is that right?"* He said, *"Yes,"* and then told us his name. I said, *"You have a New Testament you use, don't you?"* *"Oh, yes,"* he said. I asked, *"On which Greek text is your New Testament based?* Are you familiar with the so-called Westcott-and-Hort-type-text?" *"Oh, yes,"* Then he said,

"We use the Received Text; we have no confidence at all in the Westcott and Hort text."

That was an interesting statement to me. **The Greek Orthodox Church still goes back to the text that underlies the KING JAMES BIBLE.**

4. Historical Evidences for the Traditional *Textus Receptus* Kind of Words During the Early Modern Period (1453--1831 A.D.)

18. The churches of the Reformation all used the Textus Receptus Kind of Words.

19. The Erasmus Greek New Testament (1516) used the Textus Receptus Kind of Words.

20. The Complutensian Polyglot (1522) used the Textus Receptus Kind of Words.

A Roman Catholic Cardinal named Ximenes, edited this edition, yet it was based, not on the texts which most Roman Catholic Bibles used, the Westcott and Hort critical text, but on the *Textus Receptus* Kind of Words.

21. Martin Luther's German Bible (1522) used the Textus Receptus Kind of Words.

22. William Tyndale's Bible, (1525), used the Textus Receptus Kind of Words.

Tyndale was a great Bible translator who was martyred because he dared to translate the Bible into English.

23. The French Version of Oliveton (1535) used the Textus Receptus Kind of Words.

24. The Coverdale Bible (1535) used the Textus Receptus Kind of Words.
25. The Matthews Bible (1537) used the Textus Receptus Kind of Words.
26. The Taverners Bible (1539) used the Textus Receptus Kind of Words.
27. The Great Bible (1539-41) used the Textus Receptus Kind of Words.
28. The Stephanus Greek New Testament (1546-51) used the Textus Receptus Kind of Words.
29. The Geneva Bible (1557-60) used the Textus Receptus Kind of Words.
30. The Bishops' Bible (1568) used the Textus Receptus Kind of Words.
31. The Spanish Version (1569) used the Textus Receptus Kind of Words.
32. The Beza Greek New Testament (1598) used the Textus Receptus Kind of Words.

That is the Greek text that the KING JAMES BIBLE was based on, using the 1598, 5th edition of Beza.

33. The Czech Version (1602) used the Textus Receptus Kind of Words.
34. The Italian Version of Diodati (1607) used the Textus Receptus Kind of Words.
35. The KING JAMES BIBLE (1611) used the traditional Textus Receptus Words.
36. The Elzevir Brothers' Greek New Testament (1624) used the Textus Receptus Kind of Words.
37. The Textus Receptus of Today Is the Same as the Original Greek New Testament Words.

This text and these Words have survived in continuity from the beginning of the New Testament itself. It is the only accurate representation of the original Greek Words that we have today!

Personal Conviction on Bible Words

In fact, it is my own personal conviction and belief, after studying this subject since 1971, that the Words of the Received Greek and Masoretic Hebrew texts that underlie the King James Bible are the very Words which God has preserved down through the centuries, being the exact Words of the originals themselves. As such, I believe they are inspired Words. I believe they are Preserved Words. I believe they are inerrant Words. I believe they are infallible Words. This is why I believe so strongly that any valid translation must be based upon these original language Words, and these alone!

N. The Radical Text of Westcott and Hort.

The *Textus Receptus* or Received Text was "*received by all*" until German Rationalism began to doubt it late in the 1700's and early in the 1800's. In 1881, Anglican Bishop Westcott and Professor Hort came along with a new Gnostic-based Greek text for the English Revised Version (ERV) of 1881.

The T.R.--Accepted by the Churches

The Received Text was certainly accepted by the churches down through the corridor of history. But all at once, these two men had a powerful influence by means of Hort's *Introduction* to the Greek New Testament. This book, though based on pure untested hypothesis, swayed most people of the so-called scholarly world. Everything had to change. The Received Greek Text was under fire. At first, all the preachers studied out of this false Greek text, the Westcott-and-Hort-type text (now called either the Nestle/Aland or United Bible Societies texts) but preached out of the King James Bible which was based on a different Greek text. This was a little hypocritical, but it didn't seem to bother those who practiced it. It seems like these people who do this will do most anything to keep the money and support of the fundamentalists who favor the King James Bible.

But after a while the publishers began to get "*itchy palms*." They wanted to make more money. To do this, they had to change the King James Bible itself into English versions based on this false Gnostic Greek text. Also, some of the ones who were professors, teachers, preachers, and theologians said, in effect,

"Isn't it a little inconsistent to use this Westcott and Hort Greek text and still cling to the KING JAMES BIBLE which is not based on the same Greek text?"

For many years (from 1948 through 1953) I was told by various professors at the Dallas Theological Seminary, where I attended, that I should use the American Standard Version of 1901 (not the New American Standard Version of 1960. They pushed it and said it was the best version to use. I never got it through my head why it was better. They said, "*Oh, it is better, for the King James is not as good, not as accurate.*" The reason they told me to use the American Standard Version of 1901, was because it was based on the Westcott and Hort Gnostic Greek text. They were beginning to throw out the *Received Text,* and the King James Bible. The American Standard Version of 1901, never really got off the ground. I understand that not very many people bought it. It was almost a dead issue from the start.

The Versions Follow Gnostic Words

In the chronology of important modern English versions, first, there was the English Revised Version of 1881 in England. Then there was the American Revised Version of 1898. After that, as an outgrowth of the English Revised Version of 1881, almost the same committee arranged for the American Standard Version of 1901, in this country. It followed the Westcott and Hort Gnostic Greek text. But after a while, other versions came out. The one that really began to shock and shake the world of the Evangelical Bible believers and fundamentalists was the New American Standard Version of 1960.

That is when everybody got into the act and said, in effect:

"Well, I guess the time has come to be logical and reasonable, to put the critical Greek text into the English and let us have the New American Standard Version."

But the way they sold it was **not** to admit they were changing the traditional received New Testament Greek Words in over 8,000 places, **nor** to admit they were changing the traditional Masoretic Hebrew Words and using something else. They didn't sell it on that basis. They sold it on the basis that you couldn't understand the King James Bible.

As far as Readability Index is concerned, here are some levels for the King James Bible based on the computer English program "Right Writer."

The KJB Is Very Readable

For Genesis 1	Readability = 8.13	8th Grade
For Exodus 1	Readability = 7.94	8th Grade
For Romans 1	Readability = 9.74	10th Grade
For Romans 3:1-23	Readability = 5.63	6th Grade
For Romans 8	Readability = 7.72	8th Grade
For Jude 1	Readability = 10.11	10th Grade

This certainly puts the lie to the charge that the King James Bible is too difficult to understand. This "Right Writer" readability index can be found out for any chapter or verse in the King James Bible.

The man who led me to the Lord Jesus Christ was a custodian in my high school, Uncle Charles Allen, who never went through the fifth grade. He understood the King James Bible and led me to Christ by using it when I was a high school senior. I know many people whose intelligence and educational levels have not reached as high as some of these high and mighty people who say they can't understand this King James Bible, yet these people do understand it. How do you figure that out? They say you can't understand it, that it is outmoded. Can't you understand John 3:16? Listen to it:

"For God so loved the world, that He gave His only begotten Son, that whosoever believeth in Him should not perish, but have everlasting life."

What is difficult about that? I observed a few years ago a program from mentally challenged children from the Shepherd's Home. In their presentation, they memorized all of their Bible verses from the King James Bible. Why can't the rest of the people understand it who might have attended grade school, elementary school, high school, college, graduate school, and/or seminary? But that was the way it was sold. Publishers said that the new translation makes the Bible so much easier to understand.

The Unsaved Cannot Understand

Remember 1 Corinthians 2:14 which states:

"But the natural man receiveth not the things of the Spirit of God: for they are foolishness unto him: neither can he know them, because they are spiritually discerned."

This verse is still true, regardless of which translation is used!

Our son, D. A. Waite, Jr., has written an excellent book entitled *The Comparative Readability of the Authorized Version* (**BFT #2671 @ $6.00 + $3.00 S&H**). Using computer print-outs, he compared six modern English versions with current readability standards. The six versions compared to the King James Bible were the ASV, RSV, NASV, NIV, NKJV, and NRSV. In almost every comparison, the King James Bible was slightly more readable than the other versions. I recommend that you get a copy of this book for yourself.

O. How I Got the Thirty-seven Links Supporting the Traditional *Textus Receptus* Kind of Greek Words.

There is an interesting background story of how I got together the thirty-seven historical links for the traditional *Textus Receptus* kind of Greek Words. One of the deacons from a church in Michigan asked me to find this out for him. The pastor wanted to have a man who could represent the Received Text and the King James Bible, because his church was in the midst of a controversy over what Bible they should use. Some of the intelligentsia there wanted to introduce the New International Version into the church. The pastor had been there about twenty-three years and always preached from the King James Bible. He didn't want to change. These NIV people, who were teachers in the Christian school, began to foment trouble. So the Pastor said to the deacons, in effect:

"I don't often do this as pastor, but in this one instance I will do this: You can bring a man, whomever you want from the Grand Rapids Baptist Seminary [which was a GARBC-approved school] *or wherever you want. He can talk to your deacons about the New International Version. Then I'll bring a man to talk about the Textus Receptus which underlies the Greek New Testament of the King James Bible. You deacons can listen to these men and then make up your minds and decide*

what this church is going to do."
They agreed to that. Whatever the deacons would decide, that would be the way the church would go. There would be unity. So the pastor asked me to speak. I said I would be very glad to speak. There were about eight to ten deacons in the meeting. I talked to them for a while, and then opened up the meeting for questions and answers. They had some tough questions, but I gave them the answers as well as I could. First, they were going to get a man to precede me so I could be the last word (which I would rather have had). At first, with one excuse after another, the men from Grand Rapids Baptist Seminary refused to appear. They found out I was going to be the other side of the coin and some refused to speak.

Finally, I spoke first. They changed their mind, but when their side was to show up, not one seminary man arrived, but two men. It took **two** of them to defend the New International Version and the Gnostic Westcott and Hort Greek text. When I asked them for a tape of what they had said and what their reasons were, they wouldn't give me a tape. These two men from Grand Rapids Baptist College and Seminary didn't want me to have a tape of anything they said. Do you suppose I could have answered all their arguments? I would hope so! When all was said and done, the deacons recommended that the church use only the King James Bible in all of its meetings, including the Sunday School classes. Praise the Lord! The truth (and that is what I believe we gave them) won out, at least for a while.

The Battle of Bible Versions

We're going to have battles like this all over the country. Some churches have been splitting over what Bible to use. There are many preachers who don't know what to do. They are in a quandary. They are divided between one version or another. Their church can't read a Scripture verse in unison. They have to go to the hymnbook on the screen to get something they can read together, because one will read from one version and another will read from a different one. Many pastors are sweeping this Bible version issue under the rug, hoping it will go away. It won't go away. The issue is before us. The King James Bible gives us the Words of God in English and the other versions do not. That is the simple truth.

P. The *Textus Receptus* Kind of Words Are Attested by the Evidence.

Let us see how the Words of the *Textus Receptus* are attested by the evidence. I have said that it was accepted by the churches, but what about the evidence? What evidence do we have that we can trust that these are the preserved Greek New Testament Words from which we should translate our New Testament Bibles? The evidence is divided into three groups: (1) Greek manuscripts, (2) various ancient versions or translations, and (3) the writing of the church fathers.

1. The Evidence of the Greek manuscripts. As of 1967, according to Kurt Aland in Munster, Germany, he had possession of 5,255 Greek manuscripts which have survived from apostolic times. Kurt Aland was an apostate German who didn't believe in the Words of the *Textus Receptus*, but rather in the words of the critical text. Since his death, his work is being carried on by his wife, Barbara Aland. His name is on the Nestle/Aland text. He was the chairman of the editors of that text. He has copies of many manuscripts, most of them in microfilm, (about 90% of the total available, according to one source).

Aland's Text Twists the Evidence

But every time Aland comes to a manuscript that goes along with the Words of the *Textus Receptus*, he disregards it and says it is just a copy of some other text and is not to be counted as a separate witness or as valuable. That is how Aland and his followers deal with evidence. They don't take things at face value. When they find a manuscript that agrees with the *Textus Receptus,* they say it has been doctored, *"mimeographed,"* or duplicated. Therefore, the number of texts that agree with this particular manuscript, in his mind, are not 500, 1,000, or over 5,000, but just one witness.

Aland and his followers accept the false explanation of Hort and Westcott to the effect that there was a meeting in the early church (in 250 or 350 A.D.) of all the church leaders then living. They believe, though there is not one shred of historical evidence to support this hypothesis, that these church leaders made up a revision or recension of the Greek text in which, allegedly (but falsely), all the Greek manuscripts that went along with the Westcott-and-Hort-type text were thrown out and all that went along with the *Textus Receptus* were kept. They say that everything from then on was a repetition, just like a mimeographed copy. With the result that the Words of the *Textus Receptus* manuscripts that have survived are thought to be, not independent witnesses (which, in fact, they are), but only carbon copies of but one witness.

The False "Recension" Theory

This *"recension"* theory has one problem, that is, it is just a theory. There is no proof that such a meeting or *"recension"* ever took place. Something that stupendous, where they would have called all the bishops and church fathers from all areas of the then-known world to a meeting in 250 A.D. or 350 A.D., should have left a record of some kind. But it left no historical record of any kind, yet thinking people are supposed to believe that it a fact. It is not a fact.

But that is the concoction that Professor Hort dreamed up. He had to account for the fact that in upwards of 99% or more of the 5,255 manuscripts that we have in our hands, the evidence points to the Words of the *Textus Receptus,* not to either the Westcott-and-Hort-type of text, the Nestle/Aland 26th or 27th Greek text, or the United Bible Societies text. Seeing the truth of the facts as they are, Professor Hort no doubt said to himself something like this: *"How are we going to counter this? How are we going to account for the fact that just a mere 45 documents out of 5,255, or less than 1% of the evidence now in our possession conforms to our text, while over 99% of the other evidence agrees with the Words of the Textus Receptus? Let us concoct a theory with no proof necessary. Let's say the church leaders got together and made up a recension, a text that was made to their specifications. After making it, let us say these church leaders threw out all the others and just kept their own, thus making but one recension or revision of the Greek New Testament."* That is the gist of what Professor Hort wrote in his *Introduction* to his Greek text of 1881. Though Hort's *"recension theory"* was false and completely void of any evidence, people were fooled by it and bought it. In the back of this Nestle/Aland text, there is a list of manuscripts and documents that are cited on page 711 in my copy of their 26th edition. There are about 562 manuscripts on this page. A footnote at the bottom of the page says, in Latin, **"and many others."** Since all of these manuscripts go along with the Words of the *Textus Receptus,* and really should be counted for that text, Westcott,

Hort, and Aland had to change this clear picture. They falsely counted these many witnesses as only one witness since they believe there was this special recension and all the manuscripts that agree closely are merely carbon copies of that one recension.

No "Recension" Was Ever Made

Let me repeat again, as Dean Burgon has written, there is no evidence whatsoever in the history of the church that this ever took place! It must be considered false, therefore. It is a mere theory and hypothesis.

What about the manuscripts? What kinds are there? There are four kinds of Greek manuscripts that we have in our possession today: (1) papyri, (2) uncials, (3) cursives, and (4) lectionaries.

(1) Papyrus Fragment Manuscripts. The first kind of manuscript is the papyrus fragment. These are small pieces of papyrus. Papyrus is a kind of paper made out of the papyrus plant which grows plentifully in Egypt. It is brittle. Most papyri don't have many verses on them. There were eighty-one of them as of 1967. Now they have eighty-eight. Of the eighty-eight, according to an estimate by Pastor Jack Moorman in his book, *Forever Settled* [BFT #1428 @ $20.00 + $5.00 S&H], only about thirteen (**15%**) go along with "B" and Aleph, the Westcott and Hort text; about seventy-five (**85%**) of the eighty-eight go along with the Words of the *Textus Receptus*.

(2) Uncial Manuscripts. Uncials (or majuscules) are Greek manuscripts written in capital letters which are jumbled together without any breaks in the letters. There are no punctuation marks and no spaces between the letters. There are some old uncials and there are some more recent ones. Some have said that "*uncials*" means "*large or inch-long letters.*" In 1967 there were 267 uncials. Only nine of these 267 go along with the Westcott and Hort text (**only 3%**). But 258 of the 267 (**97%**) go along with the Words of the Textus Receptus.

Uncials Are Strong for the TR

By the way, when Westcott and Hort saw that only nine of the 267 uncials lined up with their text, they decided to use only the old uncials, *A, B, Aleph, C* and *D*. These are called old uncials, from the 4th century up to the 6th century. What about the others? They left them out completely because they didn't support their false Gnostic Greek words.

(3) Cursive Manuscripts. Cursives (or minuscules) are Greek manuscripts written in longhand, or cursive. Their letters flow together as our own "*cursive*" writing does today. In 1967, there were 2,764 of them that were preserved.

Cursives Are Strong for the TR

Only twenty-three of the cursive manuscripts (1%) go along with the words of the Westcott and Hort text. 2,741 cursive manuscripts (99%) go along with the Words of the *Textus Receptus* that underlies the King James Bible. That is a huge number of documents favoring the *Textus Receptus*.

That is why professor Hort had to make up his false and misleading "*recension*" theory, which was based on a series of lies that have no historical support behind it. He had to account for this discrepancy, even if it meant resorting to colossal deception and falsehood!

(4) Lectionary Manuscripts. In 1967, there were 2,143 lectionaries. The word "*lection*" comes from a Latin root meaning "*to read.*" Lectionaries were portions of Scripture in the Greek and Latin Bibles that were read in the churches on certain days. All 2,143 lectionaries (**100%**) go along with the Words of the *Textus Receptus* which underlies the King James Bible. There are no lectionaries (**0%**) that support the words of the Westcott-and-Hort-type text.

Lectionaries Are Strong for the TR

In the Roman Catholic Church and the Greek Orthodox Church they make use of lectionaries even today. They read a certain portion from the Gospels and a certain portion from the Epistles on specific days. In the early days of the church age, they took the Bibles they had and marked them up to make the lections, the exact portion which should be read for that special day. Those lectionaries are good evidence to show what manuscripts they had at that time. They either put together a lectionary themselves or they had a whole Greek New Testament and marked off these special portions to show which should be read on what day. These 2,143 lectionaries are powerful evidence in favor of the historical supremacy for the Words of the *Textus Receptus*.

The Last Twelve Verses of Mark [BFT #1139 @ $15.00 + $5.00 S&H] is the title of a book by Dean John William Burgon. It was written in 1871 and contains over 350 pages. It has been reprinted by the Dean Burgon Society (DBS) and available also from the Bible For Today. The DBS has reprinted almost 3,000 pages of books by or about Dean Burgon. He was a scholar who defended the Traditional Text which underlies our King James Bible. This book contains overwhelming evidence, from manuscripts, lectionaries, ancient versions, and quotations or allusions to Scripture from the early church fathers, proving that the last twelve verses of Mark (Mark 16:9-20) are genuine. These verses have been removed from the false Gnostic Westcott and Hort Greek text. That is one of the 5,604 places (involving over 8,000 words) that have been changed by the false Gnostic texts. A black line is put between this section and the foregoing verses in the New International Version with a note reading:

"[The two most reliable early manuscripts do not have Mark 16:9-20.]"

Mark 16:9-20 Is Genuine

The editors also put these twelve verses in a footnote in the New American Standard Version. The note questions the authenticity of these verses. These twelve verses are one of the " *lections*," or reading sections used in the early lectionaries. These exact verses (Mark 16:9-20) are the Scripture portions that were read by the "*Melchite Syrian Christians as well as by the Greeks*" on the second Sunday after Easter. Dean Burgon goes into that and proves beyond any question of a doubt that this was the reason a few manuscripts dropped this section out.

He also shows that the portion before Mark 16:9-20 (verses 1-8) was also a "*lection*" or reading section. At the beginning of verse 9 there is the word, *telos*, meaning "*end*," meaning the "*end*" of the lection. Some people wrongly took this to mean that was the "*end*" of Mark's Gospel. It doesn't mean that at all. It meant that was the end of the lection portion. In this case, it was the reading from Mark 15:43 through 16:1-8.

Mark 16:9-20--An Easter Lection

This lection was read on the second Sunday after Easter [cf. Burgon, *The Last Twelve Verses of Mark* [BFT #1139 @ $15.00 + $5.00 S&H], pp. 226, 238. [See page 238 for the other times these verses were read as a lection]. So lectionaries bear strong testimony in favor of the Words of the *Textus Receptus*. In chart form, here is a summary of the manuscript evidence (for the 1967 numbers) for the Words of the *Textus Receptus* (TR) as opposed to the words of the false Gnostic texts of Westcott and Hort, Nestle/Aland, or United Bible Societies.

The TR–Attested By the Evidence

	TOTALS:	# of MSS WH/TR	% of MSS WH/TR
Papyrus Fragments	81(88)	13/75	15%/85%
Uncials	267	9/258	3%/97%
Cursives	2764	23/2741	1%/99%
Lectionaries	2143	0/2143	0%/100%
TOTALS:	**5,255**	**45/5217**	**1%/99%**

2. The Evidence of the Ancient Versions or Translations. The ancient versions are translations of the Greek Bible from the earliest times. For instance, the Peshitta Syriac, second century, about 150 A.D., is strongly based on the Words of the *Textus Receptus.* The Curetonian Syriac, third century, is also based basically on the Words of the *Textus Receptus.* The Old Latin, or *Vetus Itala*, of the second century A. D. is also largely from the Words of the *Textus Receptus.* In the other versions that are available, some take the Words of the *Textus Receptus,* some do not. **But these are evidences.**

3. The Evidence of the Church Fathers. The church fathers were early church writers such as bishops, pastors, and other church leaders who wrote letters to the churches in the early days of the church. In the course of their writings, they often either alluded to verses of Scripture or quoted those verses exactly.

Church Fathers Quotes for the T.R.

These church fathers were quoting or alluding to verses found either in their Greek or Latin New Testaments, They either quoted the verses verbatim, or made reference in some way to the verses. From some of those allusions or quotations, you can tell what kind of Bible text they had in their hand. Was it the words of the Westcott and Hort text, or was it the Words of the *Textus Receptus*?

Dean John William Burgon, is the author of these five books which the Dean Burgon Society (DBS) has reprinted in hardback editions:
1. *The Revision Revised* [BFT #611 @ $25.00 + $5.00 S&H],
2. *The Last 12 Verses of Mark* [BFT #1139 @ $15.00 + $5.00 S&H],
3. *The Traditional Test of the Holy Gospels* [BFT #1159 @ $15.00 + S&H],
4. *The Causes of Corruption of the Holy Gospels* [BFT #1160 @ $16.00 + $5.00 S&H], and
5. *Inspiration and Interpretation* [BFT #1220 @ $25.00 + $5.00 S&H].

Dean Burgon's Sound Books

In these books, Dean Burgon goes into great detail on the matter of the church fathers. Before he died in 1888, Dean John William Burgon and his staff amassed more then 86,000 quotations or allusions to Scripture by the early church fathers. This documentation still exists today in the British Museum Library in London, England. The research is contained in sixteen large folio volumes.

One of the members of our Dean Burgon Society Executive Committee, Dr. Jack Moorman, one of our church's missionaries in England, gave me a report on these volumes in his letter of January 10, 1992.

He wrote that each of the sixteen volumes was about ten inches by twelve and one-half inches in size. They are five inches to seven inches thick. You can well imagine the hundreds of hours that went into that research on the part of Dean Burgon and his staff to produce sixteen volumes of that size. It is unfortunate that these were not published in a more permanent manner. They are in handwritten form only. Dr. Moorman wrote:

"They are . . . an _index_ to quotations in _other_ works, mainly that of J. P. Migne. The volumes are all references: there are no quotations from the Fathers. . . . The references are handwritten on small slips and pasted on the pages in Biblical order under a given Father. Each slip contains the chapter and verse of the Scripture, followed by the volume and page in a patristic edition where that text is quoted. I assume that there are some 86,000 slips in the sixteen volumes. . ."

This letter was a valuable report on the present status of this research on the church fathers and their allusions to the New Testament Scriptures.

The quotations showed what kind of Greek text the church fathers were using. There were many allusions made to the received or traditional Text. From 100-300 A. D. there were approximately 100 church fathers who wrote extensively and referred in some way to the New Testament verses. From 300-600 A. D. there were approximately 200 fathers who wrote extensively. So there are 300 church fathers who wrote from 100 A.D. to 600 A.D. You can quite often look at the writings and see which text they had in their hands, whether the *Textus Receptus* or the so-called "*neologian*" or critical text of the Vatican ("B") and Sinai (Aleph) words favored by Westcott and Hort.

Edward Miller edited Dean Burgon's work, because Burgon died before he could complete his massive study on the New Testament text. In 1896, Miller published two of Burgon's books, one of which was *The Traditional Text of the Holy Gospels*. [BFT #1159 @ $15.00 + $5.00 S&H] In it is a list of church fathers who quoted different portions of the Words of the *Textus Receptus* and a list of those who quoted from the Westcott-and-Hort-type of words. This list (on pages 99-100) contains the names and records of seventy-six writers who died before 400 A. D.

Fathers' Quotes Strong for the T.R.

1. It shows the impressive number of quotations from the Words of the traditional text. Miller found the following facts:

2. There were quotations from the Words of the traditional text (*Textus Receptus*) from church fathers who died in 400 A.D. or before;

3. The Words of the traditional text quotations were in the majority over those favoring the words of the "*neologian*" (Westcott-Hort-type) text; and also

4. The Words of the traditional text quotations were in the ratio of 3 to 2 (60% to 40%) in their favor!

Of a total of 4,383 quotations from the seventy-six church fathers who died before 400 A.D., there were 2,630 (60%) of the quotations from the Words of the traditional or *Textus Receptus* and only 1,753 (40%) of the quotations from the words of the "*neologian*" or Westcott-Hort-type of text. This is a ratio of 3 to 2 or 1.5 to 1 in favor of the Words of the traditional or Textus Receptus.

T.R. Words From the Beginning

Today, writers of the Gnostic Westcott and Hort school frequently make the false statement that there are no references to the Words of the traditional or *Textus Receptus* before the fourth century. These figures certainly prove them in error.

.

Dr. Moorman's sixth book on the subject of the New Testament text was entitled *Early Church Fathers And The Authorized Version--A Demonstration-- Companion Volume To Early Manuscripts And The Authorized Version.* [BFT #2136 @ $6.00 + $3.00 S&H] This is an excellent book that our readers will want to acquire. He used a more recent reference source for both the Nicene and Post-Nicene church fathers. He examined eighty-six different works from church fathers who died from 110 to 397 A.D. (before 400 A.D.). He compared 401 Scripture quotations cited in the Digest source. He found 279 to refer to the Words of the *Textus Receptus* and only 114 or 122 to refer to the words of the Vatican ("B") and Sinai (Aleph)--Westcott/Hort, Nestle/Aland, or United Bible Societies type of texts. This is a ratio of 2.3 to 1 as over against 1.5 to 1 found by Burgon and Miller--a much higher ratio! We appreciate Pastor Moorman's excellent scholarship in New Testament textual matters.

This study has now been put in a hardback book entitled *Early Manuscripts, Church Fathers, and the Authorized Version* [BFT #3230 @ $20.00 + $5.00 S&H]. This is indeed a useful book to have and read.

Q. An Evaluation of the Gnostic Vatican ("B") and Sinai (Aleph) Manuscripts. The two Gnostic manu-

scripts that the Westcott and Hort (and NA and UBS) followers rely upon are the Vatican ("B") and Sinai (Aleph) manuscripts. These manuscripts originated in Alexandria, Egypt. They are presumably fourth century uncials which had very little, if any, use by their owners. I believe this was true because the owners recognized them to be perverted texts, having been defaced and polluted by Gnostic heretics and others in Alexandria, Egypt where they originated.

Vatican & Sinai MSS Are False

Westcott & Hort and their followers say that the Vatican and Sinai manuscripts are superior merely because they are the oldest and therefore purest. They are neither the best nor the purest. They were corrupted by the Gnostic heretics whose headquarters were in Alexandria, Egypt.

Why Gnostic MSS Were Preserved

I believe there are at least two reasons for these two documents being preserved.

1. The first reason they were preserved is they were in Egypt where the climate was conducive to their survival.

2. The second reason they were preserved is that they were not used by the church because they realized they were full of Gnostic heretical changes. These copies happened to escape the burnings and persecutions in the early church, perhaps, by being hidden away through disuse and not out in the open.

If they had been used, they would have been worn out like my first leather Bible, which is just about in tatters. My wife gave it to me in 1947, the year before we were married. I'm using it, and have had it rebound several times. When you use a book constantly, it gets tattered and torn.

The Vatican manuscript ("B") was stored in the Vatican library in the Roman Catholic Vatican. The Sinai manuscript (Aleph) was found in a wastepaper basket at St. Catherine's Monastery.

. They were getting ready to burn it to keep warm for the winter or to cook their meal. There was a very comical expression that my fellow-debater used when we were debating Dr. Stuart Custer (of Bob Jones University) and his partner, Dr. James Price (of Tennessee Temple College) on the Greek manuscripts. My partner, Dr. James Qurollo, had a very interesting way of putting it. Tischendorf was the one who bought this manuscript from St. Catherine's Monastery. He was a German apostate scholar who was working on the New Testament. He bought it for hundreds and hundreds of dollars from the monks who were getting ready to burn it. Dr. Qurollo said,

"I don't know which of them had the truer evaluation of its worth--Tischendorf, who wanted to buy it, or the monks, who

were getting ready to **burn** *it!"*

Tischendorf had to pay dearly for what was considered by the monks to be "trash." It really was that, because of all the Gnostic heretical perversions. After he found this Sinai (Aleph) manuscript in the wastebasket, Tischendorf went back and altered his old editions of the Greek New Testament in hundreds of places, completely revolutionizing it after it had been completed. Dean Burgon's *Revision Revised* [BFT #611 @ $25.00 + $5.00 S&H] has an excellent analysis of the defects both of the Vatican ("B") and the Sinai (Aleph) manuscripts. Another excellent analysis of these two Gnostic documents can be found in a book by Cecil J. Carter entitled *The Oldest And Best Manuscripts--How Good Are They?* [BFT #1733 @ $7.00 + $3.00 S&H] He cites Tischendorf as reporting that the Sinai (Aleph) manuscript contained **"15,000 changes made by contemporary or later hands"** (p. 10). Consider the defects that must have abounded in the Gnostic Sinai (Aleph) manuscript to have needed 15,000 changes by various correctors!

Westcott/Hort's Worship of Vatican

Professor Hort, in his *Introduction* to his and Bishop Westcott's new Greek text of 1881, said that the readings of "B" and Aleph, where they agreed, were the true readings of the New Testament. If they did not agree, then any binary (or combination of two) readings of "B" with one other manuscript would be the true reading.

If they could not find any other manuscript to agree with "B" (Vatican), then B alone would be sufficient to establish the true reading. It is quite evident that they had a strong prejudice in favor of "B." H. C. Hoskier's two volume book on *CODEX B AND ITS ALLIES* has been reprinted by the BIBLE FOR TODAY. [BFT #1643 @ $46.00 + $9.00 S&H] Hoskier's very technical comparison of "B" with Aleph showed these two corrupt manuscripts to be in contradiction one with the other in **over 3,000 places in the Gospels alone!** In other words, if "B" is right, Aleph is wrong. If Aleph is right, "B" is wrong. It is quite possible, in these instances, that NEITHER "B" nor Aleph is correct.

Vatican & Sinai Not the "Oldest"

It is mainly the Gnostic Vatican manuscript ("B") which Westcott and Hort relied upon. It was supposedly written in 350 to 375 A.D. They just about worshiped that manuscript. Burgon and Miller came along, with over 86,000 quotations from the church fathers, many of which antedated either "B" or Aleph. Dr. Moorman did further research along the same lines, as mentioned above. If indeed the "*oldest is the best*," Westcott and Hort are beaten at their own game.

The church fathers thereby demolish the arguments of B and Aleph of the 4th century because the fathers go back before even the 4th century and bear witness to a much earlier text than either B or Aleph. As mentioned above, Burgon and Miller cited seventy-six church fathers who wrote and who died before 400 A.D. Irenaeus, for example, lived around 150 A.D. Pastor Moorman cited eighty-six church fathers who wrote and died before 400 A.D. Ignatius, for example, died in 110 A.D. All three of his quotations were from the Traditional or *Textus Receptus* type of text. The Westcott and Hort people say a manuscript is bad because it is not old enough. They also erroneously boast that there are no *Textus Receptus* readings before 400 A.D. Yet the above evidence proves this to be in error.

T.R.–the Preponderance of Evidence

Not only were readings found from the Traditional Text, but they were found to be in the MAJORITY of cases. In other words, more than half were from the *Received Text* rather than the Westcott-and-Hort-type text. Not only did they find the Traditional Text readings to be in the MAJORITY, but to be in a PREPONDERANCE of cases, either 1.5 to 1 (Burgon & Miller) or 2.3 to 1 (Moorman) in favor of the Traditional Text rather than just a simple majority! So this is a powerful argument.

Of course Hort had an argument explaining **why** the church fathers quoted the *Received Text* more than their preferred text of "B" and Aleph. He claimed falsely that the editions of the church fathers were altered also, just like he claims the Greek manuscripts were altered in the years of about 250 to 350 A.D. As in the case of the false recension of the Greek New Testament, so in the case of the church fathers' recension, there is not a particle of evidence to prove that this ever took place! It is pure hypothesis and speculation on his part. Hort had an answer for everything, however spurious, erroneous, and bereft of a single shred of evidence or proof. The leaders of the Baptists, Presbyterians, Southern Baptists in Louisville, and many others, fell hook, line, and sinker for Hort's specious arguments. They were thoroughly deceived by a master deceiver and apostate. They apparently did not know enough to check out the evidence for themselves. They just accepted what Westcott and Hort dogmatically asserted with no proof whatever. They accepted this fanciful theory uncritically, and the entire church has been suffering for it ever since.

KJB's Greek Words Can be Trusted

Basically, I would like to say that the New Testament foundation or basis for our Greek New Testament which underlies our KING JAMES BIBLE was definitely authorized and accepted by the churches down through the centuries, attested by the evidence, and therefore absolutely worthy of being trusted and believed by us today or in any future age!

Index of Words and Phrases

About the Author

The author of this book, Dr. D. A. Waite, received a B.A. (Bachelor of Arts) in classical Greek and Latin from the University of Michigan in 1948, a Th.M. (Master of Theology), with high honors, in New Testament Greek Literature and Exegesis from Dallas Theological Seminary in 1952, an M.A. (Master of Arts) in Speech from Southern Methodist University in 1953, a Th.D. (Doctor of Theology), with honors, in Bible Exposition from Dallas Theological Seminary in 1955, and a Ph.D. in Speech from Purdue University in 1961. He holds both New Jersey and Pennsylvania teacher certificates in Greek and Language Arts.

He has been a teacher in the areas of Greek, Hebrew, Bible, Speech, and English for over thirty-five years in ten schools, including one junior high, one senior high, four Bible institutes, two colleges, two universities, and one seminary. He served his country as a Navy Chaplain for five years on active duty; pastored three churches; was Chairman and Director of the Radio and Audio-Film Commission of the American Council of Christian Churches; since 1969, has been Founder, President, and Director of THE BIBLE FOR TODAY; since 1978, has been President of the DEAN BURGON SOCIETY; has produced over 700 other studies, books, cassettes, VHS's, CD's, or VCR's on various topics; and is heard on a thirty-minute weekly radio program IN DEFENSE OF TRADITIONAL BIBLE TEXTS, on radio, shortwave, and streaming on the Internet at BibleForToday.org, 24/7/365.

Dr. and Mrs. Waite have been married since 1948; they have four sons, one daughter, and, at present, eight grandchildren, and eight great-grandchildren. Since October 4, 1998, he has been the Pastor of the 𝔅𝔦𝔟𝔩𝔢 𝔉𝔬𝔯 𝔗𝔬𝔡𝔞𝔶 𝔅𝔞𝔭𝔱𝔦𝔰𝔱 𝔠𝔥𝔲𝔯𝔠𝔥 in Collngswood, New Jersey.

Order Blank (p. 1)

Name:_____

Address:_____

City & State:_____Zip:_____

Credit Card #:_____Expires:_____

Latest Books

[ ] Send *The KJB's Superior Hebrew & Greek Words* by Pastor
D. A. Waite, 104 pp., perfect bound ($10+$4 S&H)
[ ] Send *Soulwinning's Versions-Perversions* by Pastor D. A.
Waite, booklet, 28 pp. ($5+$3 S&H) fully indexed
[ ] Send *2 Timothy--Preaching Verse by Verse*, by Pastor D. A.
Waite, 250 pages, perfect bound ($11+$5 S&H) fully indexed.
[ ] Send *A Critical Answer to God's Word Preserved* by Pastor D.
A. Waite, 192 pp. perfect bound ($11.00+$4.00 S&H)

The Most Recently Published Books

[ ] Send *8,000 Differences Between Textus Receptus & Critical Text*
by Dr. J. A. Moorman, 544 pp., hrd. back ($20+$5 S&H)
[ ] *Early Manuscripts, Church Fathers, & the Authorized
Version* by Dr. Jack Moorman, $20+$5 S&H. Hardback
[ ] Send *The LIE That Changed the Modern World* by Dr.
H. D. Williams ($16+$5 S&H) Hardback book
[ ] Send *With Tears in My Heart* by Gertrude G. Sanborn.
Hardback 414 pp. ($25+$5 S&H) 400 Christian Poems

Preaching Verse by Verse Books

[ ] Send *2 Timothy--Preaching Verse by Verse*, by Pastor D. A.
Waite, 250 pages, hardback ($11+$5 S&H) fully indexed.
[ ] Send 1 Timothy--Preaching Verse by Verse, by Pastor D. A.
Waite, 288 pages, hardback ($14+$5 S&H) fully indexed.
[ ] Send *Romans--Preaching Verse by Verse* by Pastor D. A.
Waite 736 pp. Hardback ($25+$5 S&H) fully indexed

Send or Call Orders to:
THE BIBLE FOR TODAY
900 Park Ave., Collingswood, NJ 08108
Phone: 856-854-4452; FAX:--2464; Orders: 1-800 JOHN 10:9
E-Mail Orders: BFT@BibleForToday.org; Credit Cards OK

Order Blank (p. 2)

Name:_____

Address:_____

City & State:_____Zip:_____

Credit Card #:_____Expires:_____

More Preaching Verse by Verse Books

[ ] Send *Colossians & Philemon--Preaching Verse by Verse* by
    Pastor D. A. Waite ($12+$5 S&H) hardback, 240 pages.

[ ] Send *Philippians--Preaching Verse by Verse* by Pastor D.
    A. Waite ($10+$5 S&H) hardback, 176 pages.

[ ] Send *Ephesians--Preaching Verse by Verse* by Pastor D. A.
    Waite ($12+$5 S&H) hardback, 224 pages.

[ ] Send *Galatians--Preaching Verse By Verse* by Pastor D. A.
    Waite ($13+$5 S&H) hardback, 216 pages.

[ ] Send *First Peter--Preaching Verse By Verse* by Pastor D.
    A. Waite ($10+$5 S&H) hardback, 176 pages.

Books on Bible Texts & Translations

[ ] Send *Defending the King James Bible* by DAW ($12+$5
    S&H) A hardback book, indexed with study questions.

[ ] Send *BJU's Errors on Bible Preservation* by Dr. D. A.
    Waite, 110 pages, paperback ($8+$4 S&H) fully indexed

[ ] Send *Fundamentalist Deception on Bible Preservation* by
    Dr.Waite, ($8+$4 S&H), paperback, fully indexed

[ ] Send *Fundamentalist MIS-INFORMATION on Bible Ver-*
    sions by Dr. Waite ($7+$4 S&H) perfect bound, 136 pages

[ ] Send *Fundamentalist Distortions on Bible Versions* by
  Dr.Waite ($7 3 S&H) A perfect bound book, 80 pages

[ ] Send *Fuzzy Facts From Fundamentalists* by Dr. D. A.
    Waite ($8.00 + $4.00) printed booklet

Send or Call Orders to:
THE BIBLE FOR TODAY
900 Park Ave., Collingswood, NJ 08108
Phone: 856-854-4452; FAX:--2464; Orders: 1-800 JOHN 10:9
E-Mail Orders: BFT@BibleForToday.org; Credit Cards OK

Order Blank (p. 3)

Name:_____

Address:_____

City & State:_____Zip:_____

Credit Card #:_____Expires:_____

More Books on Bible Texts & Translations

[ ] Send *Foes of the King James Bible Refuted* by DAW ($9 +$4 S&H) A perfect bound book, 164 pages in length.

[ ] Send *Central Seminary Refuted on Bible Versions* by Dr. Waite ($10+$4 S&H) A perfect bound book, 184 pages

[ ] Send *The Case for the King James Bible* by DAW ($7 +$3 S&H) A perfect bound book, 112 pages in length.

[ ] Send *Theological Heresies of Westcott and Hort* by Dr. D. A. Waite, ($7+$3 S&H) A printed booklet.

[ ] Send *Westcott's Denial of Resurrection*, Dr. Waite ($4+$3)

[ ] Send *Four Reasons for Defending KJB* by DAW ($3+$3)

More Books on Texts & Translations

[ ] Send *Holes in the Holman Christian Standard Bible* by Dr. Waite ($3+$2 S&H) A printed booklet, 40 pages

[ ] Send *Contemporary Eng. Version Exposed*, DAW ($4+$2)

[ ] Send *NIV Inclusive Language Exposed* by DAW ($7+$3)

[ ] Send *26 Hours of KJB Seminar* (4 videos) by DAW($50.00)

Books By Dr. Jack Moorman

[ ] Send Manuscript Digest of the N.T. (721 pp.) By Dr. Jack Moorman, copy-machine bound ($50+$7 S&H)

[ ] *Early Manuscripts, Church Fathers, & the Authorized Version* by Dr. Jack Moorman, $20+$5 S&H. Hardback

[ ] Send *Forever Settled--Bible Doc*uments *& History Survey* by Dr. Jack Moorman, $20+$5 S&H. Hardback book.

[ ] Send *When the KJB Departs from the So-Called "Majority Text"* by Dr. Jack Moorman, $16+$5 S&H

Send or Call Orders to:
THE BIBLE FOR TODAY
900 Park Ave., Collingswood, NJ 08108
Phone: 856-854-4452; FAX:--2464; Orders: 1-800 JOHN 10:9
E-Mail Orders: BFT@BibleForToday.org; Credit Cards OK

Order Blank (p. 4)

Name:_____

Address:_____

City & State:_____Zip:_____

Credit Card #:_____Expires:_____

More Books By Dr. Jack Moorman

[ ] Send *Missing in Modern Bibles--Nestle-Aland/NIV Errors* by Dr. Jack Moorman, $8+$4 S&H

[ ] Send *The Doctrinal Heart of the Bible--Removed from Modern Versions* by Dr. Jack Moorman, VCR, $15 +$4 S&H

[ ] Send *Modern Bibles--The Dark Secret* by Dr. Jack Moorman, $5+$3 S&H

[ ] Send *Samuel P. Tregelles--The Man Who Made the Critical Text Acceptable to Bible Believers* by Dr. Moorman ($2+$1)

[ ] Send *8,000 Differences Between TR & CT* by Dr. Jack Moorman [$20 + $5.00 S&H] a hardback book

[ ] Send *356 Doctrinal Erors in the NIV & Other Modern Versions*, 100-large-pages, $10.00+$6 S&H.

Books By or About Dean Burgon

[ ] Send *The Revision Revised* by Dean Burgon ($25 + $5 S&H) A hardback book, 640 pages in length.

[ ] Send *The Last 12 verses of Mark* by Dean Burgon ($15+$5 S&H) A hardback book 400 pages.

[ ] Send *The Traditional Text* hardback by Burgon ($15+$5 S&H) A hardback book, 384 pages in length.

[ ] Send *Causes of Corruption* by Burgon ($16+$5 S&H) A hardback book, 360 pages in length.

Send or Call Orders to:
THE BIBLE FOR TODAY
900 Park Ave., Collingswood, NJ 08108
Phone: 856-854-4452; FAX:--2464; Orders: 1-800 JOHN 10:9
E-Mail Orders: BFT@BibleForToday.org; Credit Cards OK

Order Blank (p. 5)

Name:_____

Address:_____

City & State:_____Zip:_____

Credit Card #:_____Expires:_____

More Books By or About Dean Burgon

[ ] Send *Inspiration and Interpretation*, Dean Burgon ($25+$5 S&H) A hardback book, 610 pages in length.

[ ] Send *Burgon's Warnings on Revision* by DAW ($7+$4 S&H) A perfect bound book, 120 pages in length.

[ ] Send *Westcott & Hort's Greek Text & Theory Refuted by Burgon's Revision Revised–Summarized* by Dr. D. A. Waite ($7.00+$4 S&H), 120 pages, perfect bound.

[ ] Send *Dean Burgon's Confidence in KJB* by DAW ($3+$3)

[ ] Send *Vindicating Mark 16:9-20* by Dr. Waite ($3+$3S&H)

[ ] Send *Summary of Traditional Text* by Dr. Waite ($4 +$2)

[ ] Send *Summary of Causes of Corruption*, DAW ($4+$2)

[ ] Send *Summary of Inspiration* by Dr. Waite ($4+$2 S&H)

More Books by Dr. D. A. Waite

[ ] Send *Making Marriage Melodious* by Pastor D. A. Waite ($7+$4 S&H), perfect bound, 112 pages.

Books by D. A. Waite, Jr.

[ ] Send *Readability of A.V. (KJB)* by D. A. Waite, Jr. ($6+$3)

[ ] Send *4,114 Definitions from the Defined King James Bible* by D. A. Waite, Jr. ($7.00+$4.00 S&H)

[ ] Send *The Doctored New Testament* by D. A. Waite, Jr. ($25+$5 S&H) Greek MSS differences shown, hardback

[ ] Send *Defined King James Bible* lg. prt. leather ($40+$10)

[ ] Send *Defined King James Bible* med. leather $35+$8.50)

Send or Call Orders to:
THE BIBLE FOR TODAY
900 Park Ave., Collingswood, NJ 08108
Phone: 856-854-4452; FAX:--2464; Orders: 1-800 JOHN 10:9
E-Mail Orders: BFT@BibleForToday.org; Credit Cards OK

Order Blank (p. 6)

Name:_____

Address:_____

City & State:_____Zip:_____

Credit Card #:_____Expires:_____

Miscellaneous Authors

[ ] Send *Wycliffe Controversies* by Dr. H. D. Williams, perfect bound, 311 pages @ $20.00 + $5.00 S&H

[ ] Send *The Pure Words of God* by Dr. H. D. Williams, perfect bound ($15.00 + $5 S&H)

[ ] Send *Hearing the Voice of God* by Dr. H. D. Williams, perfect bound ($18.00 + $5.00 S&H)

[ ] Send *The Attack on the Canon of Scripture* by Dr. H. D. Williams, perfect bound ($15.00 + $4.00 S&H)

[ ] Send *Word-For-Word Translating of The Received Texts* by Dr. H. D. Williams, 288 pages, paperback ($10+$5 S&H).

[ ] Send *Guide to Textual Criticism* by Edward Miller ($11+$4) a hardback book

[ ] Send *Scrivener's Greek New Testament Underlying the King James Bible*, hardback, ($14+$5 S&H)

[ ] Send *Scrivener's Annotated Greek New Testament*, by Dr. Frederick Scrivener: Hardback--($35+$5 S&H); Genuine Leather--($45+$5 S&H)

[ ] Send *Why Not the King James Bible?--An Answer to James White's KJVO Book* by Dr. K. D. DiVietro, $10+$5 S&H

[ ] Send Brochure #1: "*1000 Titles Defending the KJB/TR*" No Charge

Send or Call Orders to:
THE BIBLE FOR TODAY
900 Park Ave., Collingswood, NJ 08108
Phone: 856-854-4452; FAX:--2464; Orders: 1-800 JOHN 10:9
E-Mail Orders: BFT@BibleForToday.org; Credit Cards OK

The Defined

𝕶𝖎𝖓𝖌 𝕵𝖆𝖒𝖊𝖘 𝕭𝖎𝖇𝖑𝖊

UNCOMMON WORDS DEFINED ACCURATELY

I. Deluxe Genuine Leather

✦Large Print--Black or Burgundy✦

1 for $40.00+$10.00 S&H

✦Case of 12 for✦

$30.00 each+$35 S&H

✦Medium Print--Black or Burgundy ✦

1 for $35.00+$8.50 S&H

✦Case of 12 for✦

$25.00 each+$25 S&H

II. Deluxe Hardback Editions

1 for $20.00+$10.00 S&H (Large Print)

✦Case of 12 for✦

$15.00 each+$35 S&H (Large Print)

1 for $15.00+$7.50 S&H (Medium Print)

✦Case of 12 for✦

$10.00 each+$25 S&H (Medium Print)

Order Phone: 1-800-JOHN 10:9

Pastor D. A. Waite, Th.D., Ph.D.

The King James Bible's Original Words

- **The Background of This Booklet.** The idea for this booklet came from my book, *Defending The King James Bible* (**BFT #1594 @ $12.00 + $4.00 S&H**). In this book, I point out four superiorities of the King James Bible: It has (1) superior texts, (2) superior translators, (3) superior translation technique, and (4) superior theology. I have simply taken point #1 and edited it for printing here.

- **The Need For This Booklet.** One of the most important parts of the battle for the real Bible in our time is the answer to the question: Which Old Testament Hebrew and Aramaic Words and which New Testament Greek Words are we to use as the basis for all our translations? Since there are so many viewpoints on this, there is a drastic need to discuss the problem in detail.

- **The Purpose of This Booklet.** In this booklet, I attempt to meet the need to talk about this matter and to give my reasons why I believe that the Hebrew, Aramaic, and Greek Words underlying the King James Bible are the only Words that should be used as the basis for Bible translations. Though it is a complex subject, I hope I might make it clear to the readers.

- **The Use of This Booklet.** I will be using this booklet at two upcoming meetings. One meeting will be at an independent Baptist college. The other will be at a Bible conference in Mexico. I hope it will be used by hundreds and even thousands of God's people who need answers to this vitally important problem.

www.BibleForToday.org

BFT 3384   **ISBN #1-56848-062-8**